The Book of Shadows

The
Book
of
Shadows

The Unofficial
Charmed
Companion

N. E. GENGE

 THREE RIVERS PRESS • NEW YORK

This book has not been prepared, licensed, endorsed, or in any
way authorized by any entity that created or produced *Charmed*.

Published by Three Rivers Press, New York, New York. Member of the Crown
Publishing Group.

Random House, Inc. New York, Toronto, London, Sydney, Auckland

www.randomhouse.com

THREE RIVERS PRESS is a registered trademark and the Three Rivers Press
colophon is a trademark of Random House, Inc.

Printed in the United States of America

Design by Lindgren/Fuller Design

Library of Congress Cataloging-in-Publication Data

Genge, N. E.
    The book of shadows : the unofficial *Charmed* companion / by N.E.
        Genge.—1st ed.
        1. *Charmed* (Television program) 2. Witchcraft. I. Title
PN1992.77C47 G46 2000
791.45′72—dc21   00-044341

ISBN 0-609-80652-1

20 19 18 17 16 15

FIRST EDITION

For my dad, Wallace Sainsbury.

1939–2000

CONTENTS

ACKNOWLEDGMENTS

It is my pleasure to thank the many terrific people who contributed something special to this project:

Patty Gift, Kieran O'Brien, and their cohorts at Three Rivers Press, who make working with them a pleasure each and every time, and who make everything I do look better. Thanks also for your compassion and flexibility during a difficult time.

Jacqueline and Mamie Sainsbury, who punched some late hours helping collect the material for this one.

Lorna Hamilton, who kept all that material organized.

Victoria Caulder, Frank and Rowan Corby, for sharing their Craft with me.

Percy McNall, for answering all my questions about magical things outside the Craft—even at bizarre hours of the night.

And, as ever, Peter and Michael, who not only put up with my schedule but hand out huge gobs of love and support in spite of it.

The Book of Shadows

The
Power of Three

Assuming you didn't tune into *Charmed* only to catch a glimpse of Shannen Doherty's admittedly attractive navel, you must have had some interest in the show's subject matter—magic.

Certainly, any number of outspoken groups, from the New Advocates for Christian Television to self-proclaimed covens, were waiting to see what Aaron Spelling would bring to the screen. *Charlie's Witches*, perhaps? It was difficult to say whether traditional church groups or proponents of the so-called New Age philosophies were more dismayed by *that* image.

Margaret Stamp, one of the many reviewers who added their comments to not-my-kids!.com, a Web site devoted to "steering impressionable youth away from the demonic influences lurking in our everyday world," had this to say of a program she had yet to even see:

I am absolutely dismayed to learn that this television network would conspire to sneak devil worship into our homes! Isn't it bad enough that Satanists are moving out of the crack houses and broken homes into decent neighborhoods? I'm already walking with a Keep Our Streets for Christ group four nights a week! Do I have to put special contraptions on my TV now, too, so they don't just beam themselves right into my living room?

A message by Teen-Witch, posted during an AOL on-line discussion took a diametrically opposed, if equally fervent, position on the upcoming show.

. . . It's not like it's not hard enough being a Wiccan to start with. People wondering if you're going to hex them or steal their babies or whatever. Now, this show'll have people wondering how many of us are out there after all, figuring that if there's enough of us to make an audience in the first place, there's probably too many of us! It's going to stir up a lot of stuff—and it probably won't know anything about real Wicca anyway!

A quick glance from the uninitiated sees only the inverted pentagram and happily assumes evil. Closer contemplation reveals the Eastern Star, with the symbols of five brave biblical women.

Fortunately for *Charmed*'s longevity, comments of the first variety faded away fairly quickly, and while critics of the second type may continue to disparage the program for "inaccurately portraying the Wiccan religion," as alleged by Teen-Witch's supporters, they at least concede that no deliberate harm is being done by the show's production. In fact, as the show continues to evolve on-screen, the real question may be whether *Charmed* is about witchcraft at all.

What?!

The show has witches and spells and potions and everything, you say. True, but to even imply that *Charmed*'s version of magic is a reflection of either modern Wicca or the older practices commonly referred to as witchcraft is to ignore some rather salient points.

For starters, what's with these special powers? Not only the Charmed Ones, but every witch they've run into, has an innate "power" of some sort. Even Aviva, the wanna-be witch in "The Fourth Sister" was given a power by her patroness, in her case a form of pyrokinesis. Any traditional witch is going to start shaking her head before you even finish the question. That's for superheroes, not witches. Wonder Woman was born an Amazon, Spiderman had his radioactive arachnid, and Superman, well, he was out of this world, but witches—as any witch, regardless of her tradition, will tell you—have to *work* for their knowledge and power. Witches aren't born with supernatural powers of any kind. Witches aren't *born* at all. That five- or six-year-olds should command such power, as portrayed in "That '70s Episode" and "Morality Bites," goes against everything most witches believe. Telekinesis, clairvoyance, astral projection, and all the rest belong rather squarely in the realm of parapsychology, and whether you believe in such talents or not, parapsychologists have been trying to separate their "science" from witchcraft, superstition, and outright hocus-pocus for nearly six decades.

Then there are all the demons that show up week after week. Demons? They may exist in a number of religions, and be tacitly nodded to by even those that don't strictly believe in them, but despite the Inquisitions and witch trials of the European Middle Ages, the style of demon common on *Charmed* was created in the minds of Christians. There are no such beasties in any version of witchcraft or Wicca—which, incidently, aren't synonymous terms either, but more on that in just a minute.

Now, add some white-lighters, a couple of dark-lighters to even out the karmic balance, some disincarnate ghosts, and a cadre of shape-shifters, and you'll have moved firmly into the land of myth and fable, some of it decidedly made-for-television fable at that. For more traditional monsters, *Charmed* incorporates Celtic mariners and Native American wendigos into its *Book of Shadows*. All of this seems far removed from the sphere of witches and Wiccans, who are, after all, merely human.

What is left, then, for all the fans who thought they were tuning in to a show about witches, sisterhood, and magic? Does *Charmed* ultimately offer them little more than *The X-Files* with a way cooler wardrobe department?

Oddly enough, despite all the extraneous gewgaws and sparkly special effects, a core of practice remains that speaks to precisely the audience that wasn't looking for belly buttons or biceps—though those touches are nice too.

But is it Wiccan practice being portrayed in prime time—as the show has always contended—or is it something else?

For an answer to that question, it's probably best to begin at the beginning with the premiere episode, "Something Wicca This Way Comes." With its title alone, the writers, producers, and network made a strong statement that this show was indeed about Wiccans. They could have followed the pattern of dozens of other shows and called their first episode the deadly dull, but literal, "Pilot," but they didn't. The content of the first episode made some fairly strong assertions as well. Information on everything that witches *weren't* poured from the character of Andy Trudeau, while his partner and the reasonable middle sister, Piper, played Joe and Jane Average, asking all the dumb questions and making all the stereotypical allusions to "conical hats." To anyone with even a basic understanding of modern Wicca, *Charmed* was starting to sound pretty solid.

Within the series's first twenty minutes, it had established its basic beliefs, to which few Wiccans would take exception.

- Most Wiccans maintain an altar space within which they practice their arts and maintain their magical implements.
- Wiccan holidays are sabbats.
- An athame is a magical implement for directing energy.
- While most Wiccans work within groups called covens, solitary practitioners do exist.
- The *Book of Shadows* is a general title for a Wiccan's magical workbook.
- A warlock isn't a male witch but an evil one.
- Triple powers have special properties.
- The Wiccan Rede, in short form, at least, is "An it harm none, do what ye will."

In fact, on that last point, the very first spell that Phoebe Halliwell undertakes is an adaptation of concepts and language in "The Witches Creed," a poem published by Doreen Valiente in her book *Witchcraft for Today*.

First, from the series:

The Power of Three
Spell from
Charmed

Hear now the words of the witches,
The secrets we hid in the night.
The oldest of gods are invoked here,
The great work of magic is sought.
In this night and in this hour,
I call upon the ancient power.
Bring your powers to we sisters three,
We want the power.
Give us the power.

Compare that with these excerpts from Valiente:

The Witches' Creed

Hear now the words of the witches,
The secrets we hid in the night,
When dark was our destiny's pathway,
That now we bring forth into the light.

. . . .

This world has no right then to know it,
And world of beyond will tell naught,
The oldest of Gods is invoked there,
The Great Work of Magic is wrought.

. . . .

And Do What You Will be the challenge,
So be it in love that harms none,
For this is the only commandment.
By magick of old be it done!

Phoebe will eventually quote a variation of those last two lines as the Wiccan Rede—"An it harm none, do what ye will." And these words are, in turn, closely related to "Rede Of The Wiccae (Being Known As The Counsel Of The Wise Ones)," which was published in *Green Egg Magazine* in 1975 by Lady Gwen Thompson, who claimed it was given to her by her grandmother Adriana Porter, from an anonymous (or secret) author's entry in a *Book of Shadows* kept within the family. The last line of the poem reads:

> 26. Eight words the Wiccan Rede fulfill—
> an it harm none, do what ye will.

As many claim that the "Rede Of The Wiccae" can be traced to a period pre-1935, *Charmed's* source material would seem to be a sound, historically accurate connection to ancient Wiccan traditions. Of course, that assumption presumes there were ancient

The triskela that adorns the cover of the Halliwells' *Book of Shadows* and Kit's collar is symbolic of many triple entities and tripart philosophies. "Something Wicca This Way Comes" identifies the three parts of magic as "…timing, feeling, and the phases of the moon." Other triplet associations include Wicca's Maiden, Mother, and Crone; the Celtic daughters of Fiachna, Banba, Eriu, and Fodla; and even the Christian godhead of Father, Son, and Holy Ghost. The trinity symbol enclosed within a circle echoes reincarnation, a decidedly firm belief among many traditional witches and one on the rise among Wiccans.

This variation of the triskela (see above), also known as the triquetra, adorns several Irish grave markers dating to 4 B.C. — and the skin of a frozen female mummy, believed to be a shaman, recently reinterred in its Mongolian grave.

Wiccans in the first place, which is where the whole Wicca vs. witchcraft argument begins.

While the word wicca (or wiccae) is known to exist in Old Saxon and mean, at least roughly, magic worker, it seems to have fallen out of use until the mid-1930s, when Gerald Gardner began assembling his thoughts and philosophies (many drawn from mythology, folklore, and magical societies like the famous Order of the Golden Dawn) and brought these practices together under the term Wicca. He claimed that this order was a continuation of the Old Religion of Britain. (Which makes the dating of "The Rede of the Wiccae" important to Wicca's defendants and detractors alike.) Others, however, claimed their own traditions, which they called witchcraft, were the direct religious descendants of old Britain. Both groups continue to consider each belief a complete religion quite separate from the other.

Yet, even among groups claiming similar beliefs, there are differences in the level of tolerance for one another and even the degree to which they deem a practice a separate religion. Some followers of witchcraft deplore the Wiccan use of terms like craft or witch; a significant percentage of both groups practice no magic whatsoever; and a growing group of Wiccans define themselves in terms of multiple belief systems, for example Christian-Wiccans, a concept that would be strongly denied as even a remote possibility by the traditional witches or Wiccans.

Perhaps because both groups practice much of their ritual work in private—and because some groups deliberately smudge the line between the practices, to either promote the belief that Wicca *is* older than it appears, and more worthy of serious consideration; or to make the two groups appear larger and more cohesive, and more worthy of serious consideration—there's a public perception that all Wiccans are witches and that all witches follow the same beliefs.

Wrong.

But the perception *is* convenient if you need lots of material for inspiration while writing a television program week after week. It allows, for example, the inclusion of a Siamese cat who acts suspiciously like a familiar, which, while a useful plot device, isn't a typical Wiccan accessory. It also allows a fairly broad interpretation of what magic is and is not, and what the pursuit of a magical lifestyle might include. For example, although both Wicca and witchcraft consider themselves religions with their own pantheon of deities, *Charmed* plays both sides of the religious issue. Again from "Something Wicca This Way Comes":

> Ancient One of the Earth so deep,
> Master, Moon, and Sun,
> I shield you in my Wiccan way,
> Here in my circle round,
> Asking that you protect this space,
> And offer your Sun force down.

This protection spell, with the phrasing "The oldest of Gods is invoked here," strongly implies a religious basis to *Charmed*'s magical workings. "I've Got You Under My Skin" explores that issue more when Piper begins to wonder if her newfound status as a witch means she's now persona non grata at Christian churches.

It doesn't. "When Good Warlocks Go Bad" takes that notion a step farther when a warlock takes priestly vows. By the end of that episode, the only question left is whether or not the new-made priest retained his magical abilities. As most Wiccans will say that power comes from knowledge, and knowledge can't be undone, the priesting of that particular young man merely put him outside the grasp of whatever forces were haranguing him. He must still remember everything he knew before. Other episodes of *Charmed*, such as "How to Make a Quilt out of Americans" and "The Witch Is Back," make it obvious that magical powers in the *Charmed* world can be stolen (a unique concept to both witchcraft and Wicca), but they certainly don't state, or even imply, that the practice of magical rituals negates any other religious affiliation.

Therefore, as we explore *Charmed*'s version of magic, we'll use "witch" to mean any practitioner of magical ritual, without regard to religious union, and only as it reflects the underlying precept of all things *Charmed:* the growth and empowerment of the individual.

After all, magic, by most definitions, is the direction of individual will toward change.

The purpose of this book, then, isn't to make you an instant witch, or to deconstruct world religion, but to bring a little magic, a little self-empowerment, into our lives.

The Witches' Chest

Before we go any further, let's dispel any thoughts of tired old crones hunching over foul-smelling tinctures of bat blood and ox dung. Today's witches—the *Charmed* trio included—have gladly left the freezing moors and hair-frizzing fog to Macbeth's hags. Reflecting the sensual earthiness of nature magic, the spells and components of modern practitioners combine aromatherapy, traditional and kitchen pharmacology, and ritual visualization to heighten awareness and refine desires.

Still, despite eschewing eye of newt and wing of bat, most of the spellcaster's stock in trade isn't going to be found in the neighborhood pharmacy or in the most exotic of imported food aisles. Even apparently common components, like the petals of white roses—or their thorns—aren't as easily obtained as the neophyte witch might think. Most, if not all, spell items benefit from either extreme freshness or special handling. Rose petals, for

The florist trade, like any other, has seasons and trends. White roses gain favor at Christmas and during June's weddings but lose it around Easter. Thornless roses out-perform thorned varieties at any time. Best of luck finding white, thornless roses at either the spring or fall equinoxes in smaller communities!

example, might fulfill the letter of a spell, but the process of distilling the essential oils from the freshest possible samples gives practitioners hours in which to refine not only their ingredients but the hoped-for outcome. The combination of distilled ingredients and desire vastly improves the spellcaster's chances of success.

A working component pantry, cabinet, or chest—one effective for both the beginning practitioner and the advanced occultist—must include more than a shopping list of ingredients. Knowledge, the numerous ways to heighten or modify the effect of those components, is as important an element in the witch's spiritual cabinet as any single material constituent. Don't expect to fill that cabinet in an hour, a week, even a year. Like the Power of Three and magical herbs, knowledge grows over time.

Think of the time spent accumulating these items as devotional time, a period of reflection and contemplation to consider each material's purpose in your repertoire. Will your candles benefit from anointing them with essential oils, perhaps a lavender essence to assure a child a nightmare-free night, or would a simpler treatment, like a single beeswax candle as the focus for a cleansing ritual, be more appropriate?

Some items, like meditation stones, can be adapted from other uses, especially if they hold special significance for you. If you'd like a completely fresh start, take the time to find new components, remembering that seasonal variations in your area may prevent you from gathering everything at once. Stream-washed stones bring together elements of water and earth, but obtaining them in Vermont during January might mean soaked shoes and chilled hands at best. Because each region differs in geology and ecology, you may have no natural source for seemingly common items. For this reason, review your list before you travel and keep your eyes open for treasures found in unusual places. And, while collection and preparation should be a personal endeavor, an exchange of some goods, particularly herbals, between like-minded individuals also offers surprising benefits.

Spices, Plants, and Herbals

AGRIMONY: For ensuring a deep, undisturbed—in fact, *undisturbable*—sleep, slip dried leaves of this plant inside the sleeper's

If you can't identify your edible spell components at a glance, you'd best wait a while before venturing into the realm of ingested potions! Even common ingredients can vary by location. The huge leaves to the right, for example, may bear little resemblance to the bay found on the average spice rack.

pillow. Agrimony's ready availability along the eastern seaboard makes it a handy sleep aid for children. Keep in mind that co-opting a person's free will is always questionable; indiscriminate pillow-stuffing isn't encouraged.

ARABIC, GUM: For casting a protective circle around a large area, an entire house or property—especially a circle intended to last longer than a single working—your components should be more stable and enduring than simple chalk. Gum arabic, burned in a portable censer, releases a sweet-scented smoke with which a whole structure can be censed. The same protective associations can be incorporated, on smaller scales, into myriad other types of spells by dropping small sprinkles over a brasier or into hot water.

BAY: Said to have been used by Delphic priestesses, bay, in all its parts, is a divinatory stimulant and a mild to moderate narcotic. Though it's found in most spice racks, outright ingestion isn't recommended, as bay is a well-known abortifacient; far better to use it in an incense mixture, as the Delphic oracles did.

CALAMUS: This plant has recently come under scrutiny for its beneficial effects in smoking cessation programs, but its other, more exotic, history includes nearly two thousand years of medicinal use as a stimulant and, more to the point, as an ingredient in the infamous flying ointments attributed to witches during the 1600s and 1700s.

The visible plant is pretty enough, but its power lies in the rhizomes, which are ground into a greasy base to promote the vivid flying sensations that some practitioners still consider an excellent path to astral projection and remote viewing, as well as divination.

Its aphrodisiac property makes it popular for spells to attract or renew a lover's interest.

CEDAR: Interestingly enough, the use of this plant spans several religious traditions and serves the same function in them all. The burning of small twigs, either dried or fresh, is universally associated with purification of people and their work spaces. Ritual implements also benefit from being passed through this smoke.

Magical healings routinely include censing with the smoke from cedar shavings.

Because cedar wood, oil, and incense have historic links to wealth and religious altars, buildings, and ceremonies, many witches choose this wood for the altars of their work spaces and other wooden objects. Ouija boards—or spirit boards, as they're called in *Charmed*—often feature cedar for either the board or planchette, the wooden pointer.

CENTURY PLANT: One of fifteen plants identified as magical in a 1610 manuscript, the century plant then, as now, was known for its protective qualities. Powdered, mixed with common salt (which wasn't so common in the 1600s), and cast in a circle, it turns aside the attention of ill-wishers.

(If the various explosions and puffs of smoke commonly seen on *Charmed* are any indication, the witches might well be keeping this special herb in the family pantry. Cast into a fire, the dried powder from a century plant bursts into flame, producing dense, heavy smoke that falls quickly to the floor.)

CLEAVERS: For use in spells of binding, cleavers is notable for its physically sympathetic properties. As its name implies, cleavers clings to anything and everything. Before relegating this plant to the list of things that only a warlock or other evil practitioner would traffic in, consider its use in spells that promote harmony between members of a coven and to strengthen friendship. It's also found in one of the few two-person spells, one traditionally cast between partners voluntarily joining their lives to each other.

COPAL: Not all components are meant to be consumed during everyday work; some are used to prepare other items for long-term use. Stones and crystals can become permanent parts of a witch's ritual space, used for a variety of applications. While this reuse is considered beneficial overall—stones and crystals are believed to absorb energy over time, becoming more potent with each ritual—each working is still an individual endeavor, and carrying metaphysical baggage from one working to another isn't always desirable. Copal, which burns slowly to release a scented smoke, is the "washing-up" liquid of the magical kitchen. Stones and crystals passed through the smoke receive a mystical refreshing that leaves the underlying works intact while sloughing off the associations of the last ritual.

HOLLY: Commonly used in many American traditions, holly is widely available in three different forms in eastern North America—which is good news to advanced practitioners. It is, however, toxic—bad news to neophytes. Still, used with care, in the form favored by many Native American shamans, the plant is a powerful addition to the witch's pantry. Taking the time to familiarize yourself with this component will widen your spell-casting options without endangering your health.

As an herbal medicinal, holly is sometimes linked to astringent qualities, or, like strawberry, to use as an antidiarrhetic. Unlike strawberry extract, however, the difference in dosage between medicinal and poison is far narrower. Unless you're an experienced herbalist, you might want to ignore holly's medicinal virtues in favor of its magical aspects.

Burned with incense, holly has a mildly narcotic effect. Under its relaxing influence, mental imagery is often clearer, more detailed, and more fluid. A tiny amount of the dried plant, (leaves, not berries), crushed and dusted on incense sticks before lighting or sprinkled over coals in a burner, provides the perfect degree of mental relaxation. Ritual magicians report a heightened ability to envision the magical aspects of their workings under holly's influence. Meditation is deeper, with richer imagery.

LAVENDER: In teas, sachets, or pillows, lavender serves many purposes, both banal and esoteric. Fortunately, even the nonmagical effects of this herb, often linked to the moon, can be useful to knowledgeable practitioners. Dried at the height of its fragrance (August to September, in most areas where you can grow it fresh in your own garden) and bundled into sachets, lavender permeates your work space, creating, especially for those who must work in confined or urban settings, an essential connection with the outdoors and a sensual remembrance of summer's vitality.

In an herb pillow, lavender deepens sleep, a useful effect for those whose best divination or devotional work is done during dream time. A dab of essential lavender oil on an ordinary pillow can provide similar results and, in healing magics, is highly recommended to protect young children from nightmares. Lavender tea relaxes, soothes an overexcited or troubled mind, allowing even a beginning practitioner to enter the light trance suggested for mental or spiritual exercises.

In esoteric work, lavender's associations with the moon, especially the dark of the moon, make it the ideal symbol of the practitioner's search for hidden knowledge. Mixed in dried preparation, burned as an oil, or scattered over the work surface, this plant opens the heart and mind to new experiences. Because its scent is so strongly intermingled with memory, lavendar is a favorite for those hoping to regain a connection with a younger self, or, in some cases, with a past self. Perhaps this connotation prompts its use in "That '70s Episode" as one of three ingredients burned in the Halliwell women's attic ritual space.

MISTLETOE: On one level, mistletoe's action is comprehensible to modern pharmacologists. It can cause the blood pressure to jump, often dangerously, then plummet to equally dangerous levels, all the while speeding up the heart rate. Modern chemistry, however, doesn't explain mistletoe's other traditional property—the revelation of prophetic information through visions.

MUGWORT: Used as an incense ingredient, steeped cold and hot for washing solutions and teas, dried in sleeping sachets, and fresh for the distillation of its oil, mugwort appears to be one of the most versatile herbs in the magical inventory. In all its forms, mugwort is seen as an aid to divination.

Inhaled as part of an incense mixture or, more gently, from dried leaves in a pillow, it promotes vivid dreams in even the untrained, and prophetic dreams in practitioners on lucid dreaming and those with a clairvoyant talent.

Cold infusions made from simply soaking the dried, or preferably fresh, plants in rainwater are favored cleansing agents for other divination tools such as mirrors, bowls, and balls. The same infusion, freshly made, can also be used to fill a scrying bowl.

Most often, mugwort tea is the preferred means of accessing the herb's metaphysical uses, but this method isn't for everyone. One side effect of mugwort is a well-documented incidence of birth defects. Pregnant women should avoid this plant entirely in any form, and even those who aren't pregnant should partake of it only rarely.

PEPPER: Easily culled from even the most ill-supplied kitchen, pepper in any mixture heightens awareness. Its astringent properties make it a natural for cleansing rituals; its pungent scent clears the senses and symbolizes the desire to begin fresh without emotional baggage. In "The Dream Sorcerer," Phoebe and Piper include pepper in their preparations for a spell to attract the perfect man—a prudent precaution for any spell that even hints at influencing another individual without his or her consent!

ROSEMARY: To clear away past influences and open the heart, mind, or soul for new experiences, rosemary and its essential oils are usually burned. In "Heartbreak City," Cupid adds dried rosemary to an edible potion.

SAGE: This herb, which Piper uses to try and send away her bad luck in "From Fear to Eternity," has long been considered a cleansing agent, both spiritual and physical, and it frequently appears in spells of protection and healing.

THISTLE: Relaxing medicinal teas of thistle root have been recorded for nearly seven hundred years, but in esoteric terms, thistle performs the opposite function, promoting discomfort, disorder, even chaos. Before jumping to the conclusion that this component belongs only in the spell lists of dark magicians, broaden your definition just a smidgen. A practitioner in imminent danger, whether from magical or completely human agencies, *should* feel uncomfortable.

The inclusion of thistle in any spell, including the spell cast in "That '70s Episode" to return the Halliwells to their own time, shakes up the current order before allowing it to fall into a new pattern. In the case of the sisters, displaced in time, the discomfort symbolized by thistle is their need to return to their own time and reorder past events.

In spells of protection, thistle is meant to heighten a subject's sensitivity to danger.

In a ritual designed to reveal hidden dangers, the thistle "pricks" the practitioner's awareness, providing an early warning system.

VERVAIN: If you think its other common name, enchanter's plant, hints at an arcane connection, you'd be right. Contained in medicinal and magical texts for several hundred years, it was widely believed to be as effective at turning aside magical attacks as it was in promoting healing. Unlike many other components, vervain wasn't ingested, smoked, or even dug up. Instead, it was planted around property lines and cultivated in window boxes.

Only dead plants were harvested, the naturally dried leaves crumbled to fill pocket sachets and provide the wearer with a reduced, but still helpful, level of protection.

❧ Herbal Components By Desire

Purification	Bay, broom, cedar, copal, hyssop, lemon, mint, rosemary, vervain, Saint-John's-wort
Blessings	Carnation petals, frankincense
Magical awareness	Borage, mace, mugwort, roses, star anise, yarrow
Protection	Bay, calamus, dill, fennel, frankincense, mistletoe, myrrh, pine nuts, rosemary
Spiritual awareness	Frankincense, gum arabic, sandalwood
Divination	Eyebright, mugwort, roses, wormwood, yarrow
Increased determination, bravery	Coltsfoot, thyme, yarrow
Strong friendships, coven family	Cleavers, cloves, passionflower
Simple happiness	Lavender, meadowsweet, Saint-John's-wort
Luck	Bayberry, chamomile, cinquefoil, jasmine, lotus blossoms, mint, vervain, violet
Enduring love	Basil, chamomile, cloves, ginger, roses
Physical healing	Angelica, ash bark, apple flowers, cedar, elder, sandalwood, vervain, willow
Financial rewards	Honeysuckle flowers, mace, poppy, woodruff

❧ THE WORKING ELEMENT

A Personal Growth Exercise

Ritual bathing before a magical working is common to many arcane traditions. Just as incense is cast onto charcoal to create smoke, herbal elements are scattered over bathwater to create a scent-laden mist that, like smoke, helps focus, cleanse, and prepare the practitioner. Given the set of herbals in this *Book of Shadows*, plan a bath posset to help strengthen your next magical working.

Purpose of the working:

_____

Herbals supporting the work:

_____

Oils? Fresh? Dried?

_____

Using your own associations, can you think of anything else you might add to your herbal mixture?

_____

Pungent herbs like these — nutmeg, ginger, and cinnamon — are strong memory keys, evoking solid imagery and clearing the senses.

From ritual jewelry to altar lighting, each of these objects, and an infinite number more you can locate yourself, brings the properties of earth and the individual metals to your workings.

Stones, Crystals, and Metals

If plants provide the natural element in modern witchcraft, then the inclusion of stones, crystals, and metals satisfies the desire to connect to the earth itself. Instead of the repeating cycle of birth, change, and death symbolized by plants, earth objects ground the practitioner, providing unbroken continuity. Not surprisingly, these geologic components suggest strength, determination, and constancy, in addition to the properties that have become associated with individual stones or crystals.

Stones and crystals carried on the person, in jewelry, or just slipped in a pocket, function as amulets. Crystals, even if not the crystal-ball form most commonly envisioned, can figure prominently in divination. But, like herbs and other plants, they also have a role as spell components, and we'll explore them here for that use. Likewise, small amounts of metals may be added to the witch's pantry to enhance a spell's desired end. Iron, for example, symbolizes attraction, strength, and change, characteristics of many spells, and could be added to any mixture either directly— through the inclusion of powdered iron—or indirectly, by mixing the other components in an iron vessel.

AGATE: One of the more common stones found in streams and on beaches, its colors vary widely and have given rise to a subset of magical use. The umbrella of connotations covering all agates includes bravery, longevity, healing, and protection.

AMBER: This geologically unusual stone—actually formed from plant resin—has been venerated among mystics for centuries. Transmutation is an obvious association, which likely explains its use in workings related to a change of luck, past life remembrances, and purification.

AMETHYST: Sort of a psychic cocoon, the amethyst has many esoteric connections that revolve around a central theme of healing and protection. Heightened psychic awareness, deeper meditative states, and mental tranquillity—the precursors to spiritual rejuvenation—make this stone a common ingredient in spells aimed at reestablishing a lost focus or regaining a balanced perception. As a reminder of the need for balance, an amethyst is often found in a witch's work space.

BLOODSTONE: While the amethyst might be considered mystical first aid for the battered witch soul, bloodstones are the emergency room. Along with deep healings, bloodstones carry a connotation of acceptance, even in the face of extreme adversity. Like deep pools, bloodstones act as reservoirs, holding pain aside until the practitioner can address it under less stressful circumstances. Fear, anger, and pain are lost in its depths, leaving enlightenment and peace in its wake.

COPPER: This pliable metal is fashionable now as an arthritis inhibitor, but in spell work, it symbolizes luck, love, and wealth. Whether powdered, used as a metal for magical implements and containers, or left to oxidize and grind later, copper's happy associations are welcome additions to a wide range of spell purposes.

EMERALD: More monetarily valuable than diamonds, the emerald's arcane aspects are, nonetheless, much more "down to earth." Practitioners seeking wisdom, discernment, and the ability to discriminate or deal justice might well consider adding an emerald to their list of tools.

GARNET: A historic reputation as a revealer, even neutralizer, of poisons coincides neatly with the garnet's mystical attributes. Marked as particularly reflective of higher energy, strong purposes, commitment, and courage, a garnet is appropriate in especially difficult or challenging workings.

GOLD: Generally accepted as representative of masculinity, gold can help a female practitioner achieve a more balanced perspective or heighten the self-awareness of a male practitioner. In keeping with the notion of balance, some witches place a gold object on one side of their work space and a silver object (traditionally held to be a feminine metal) opposite, to help visualize both the male and female aspects found in a single individual.

HEMATITE: Black, shiny hematite jewelry illustrates this stone's contradictory nature. Hard yet surprisingly fragile, this brittle material transforms from apparently invincible stone to fine dust with any unwary tap. It represents the need for balance and is frequently present when spells for centering, grounding, and reestablishing mental discipline are worked.

Stones serve many arcane purposes, as the accompanying list indicates. A less easily elucidated effect comes from the feel of stones or crystals in the hands. For many, the presence of these pieces soothes and comforts. At your next opportunity, take the time to carry a single piece of stone on your person for a full day. See if you don't get to like its company.

JADE: Though primarily a product of the Far East, jade is most celebrated for its magical significance in its unworked forms along the Mediterranean coasts. Alone of the many gems, stones, and crystals available to modern witches, jade is believed to facilitate astral travel not only through dreams and trance states, but through a bilocation similar in effect to that portrayed on *Charmed* as one of Prue's burgeoning abilities. Tempting as these spiritual journeys may be, jade should be included cautiously in ritual work, as it's widely held that only its geological opposite, red jasper, can ground the individual once again.

OBSIDIAN: A dark stone, obsidian represents the hidden, the obscured, the night, and the dark of the moon. Used in ritual work, it can symbolically change the time of day or the season, allowing work that might normally occur at that time to be conducted earlier or later.

OPAL: With its flashing colors obscured by a clouded matrix, opal has developed a reputation as an excellent scrying stone, the physical representation of a metaphysical endeavor. Dreaming, especially lucid dreaming, and astral projection through dreaming, are enabled through opal.

SILVER: Of all the metals, the one most associated with psychic and magical endeavors. Its linked imagery—of the moon, water, and night—reinforces that connotation. Amulets, charms, magical tools, working symbols and sigils, robe threads, and jewelry of this metal all reflect the practitioner's hope to bring the magical into contact with the physical. As a feminine metal, it balances gold's masculinity, but is particularly associated with invocation, protection, and blessings.

TIGEREYE: No doubt in response to its physical appearance and resulting name, tigereye correlates well with intuition, clairvoyance, premonitions, and the more prosaic forms of insight arising from mental stability, sound logic, and good character judgment. For a hint of something "beyond your usual ken," try using a tigereye as a scrying stone or holding it in both hands during a working.

THE WORKING ELEMENT

A Personal Growth Exercise

A comprehensive collection of crystals, gemstones, and metals can put a heavy burden on the savings account. However, since in sympathetic ritual practice one thing can stand for another, accumulating dozens of exemplars isn't necessary to begin incorporating this set of spell components into your workings.

Choose a stone, metal, or crystal:

_____

Describe the property that attracts you:

_____

_____

How might you represent that quality in other ways?

_____

_____

This is a very small sample of the numerous stones, crystals, and metals used in magical practice. Are there others that have specific meaning for you? Why might a common pebble be as valid a component as any other?

Miscellany Ordinaire

Not every spell component is specifically designed for magical use. The whole idea of "kitchen," or "granny," witches suggests that much magic is enacted outside a ritual space, a tradition reenacted in many *Charmed* episodes. "The Witch Is Back" proves the Halliwells are as comfortable casting spells from their stove as their attic altar. The inclusion of spotted owl feathers, rose thorn, thread, and even bread dough as magical ingredients in their spells suggests that their tradition was carried out in very ordinary settings with few, if any, formal restrictions.

Just some of the things to spill out of a well-stocked witch's component chest; you'll likely end up with a completely different collection before long!

Collect all the bottles you can now — you'll need them! Don't forget to include dark or opaque glass in your store: many components and potions would spoil quickly if exposed to light.

BOTTLES AND VIALS: Obviously helpful in organizing and storing other spell components, bottles can also be ingredients in and of themselves—though a spell bottle isn't always a bottle. Specially made spheres of glass or china, earthenware containers, or wooden bowls, anything that can contain your components for an extended period might qualify. Collect those that appear to reflect the properties of the components they'll be holding.

CHALK: For casting a protective circle, adding an element of earth to a working, or outlining a spiritual space, chalk is a traditional ingredient. In "Witch Trials," chalk outlines a magical doorway; in "Morality Bites," a doorway through the more prosaic material of a concrete prison wall. In "She's a Man, Baby, a Man!," a chalk circle on the floor both encloses Prue Halliwell and the *Book of Shadows*, and symbolizes the spell's intent with the shape of the traditional sign for masculinity. Chalk can also be used for written elements of spellcasting and, like ink or candles, takes on different attributes when the symbolism of various colors is incorporated. In "That Old Black Magic," the symbols that contained an evil menace were chalked in red. Red was also used to outline the pentagram enclosing the components of a lusty endeavor in "Animal Pragmatism."

CLOTH: While you may want to create a cloth that serves as a portable altar, and keep it for only that use, a supply of colored cloths for making pouches, wrapping spell components, or the ritual cleaning of other implements will also come in handy. As seen in several *Charmed* episodes, pouches often end up on a brazier, so expensive fabrics aren't necessary. Colors that reflect your usual magical practice work well.

FEATHERS: While constructing a spell that requires the feathers of an extinct or endangered bird is possible, as in "The Witch Is Back," most spell uses of feathers aren't that particular. Representing flight, freedom, and lightness, feathers bring the element of air to workings and can invoke the imagery of breezes or hurricanes. (For your further consideration: Melinda Warren cast her curse in Salem; where did *she* get a spotted owl feather?)

GLASS, COLORED: In esoteric terms, glass is often equated with a veil through which the skilled practitioner can see into other places. Crystal balls, mirrors, and the reflective surface of water serve similar purposes; colored glass can also change the quality of water or light seen through it. If you had only white tapers and an array of colored glass, you would invoke the same imagery as a practitioner with a rainbow of candles.

INK: One use of ink that has been overlooked in recent times is as a scrying aid. Poured into a bowl, it makes a dark, reflective surface that is the negative image of a container of water. Dropping small amounts of ink into pure water is another time-honored means of freeing your physical vision and concentrating on the visionary.

For the most part, however, you'll use ink for writing or illustrating your spell pages. Like candles, crystals, and glass, ink comes in many colors, and once you've given some practical thought to the archival quality of your ink—and whether or not it's going to soak through your pages—you can turn your attention to the creative aspects of inks and spellcrafting.

You can even make your own inks and paints, though these might be better used as spell components than as archival materials. Many natural sources provide the ingredients for inks, and beautiful colors can be achieved after relatively little study.

Don't be surprised if it takes you a while to find something you'd like to add to your *Book of Shadows*. Even the fictional Halliwells didn't write anything in their book until "There's a Woogy in the House."

MIRRORS: Not that long ago, mirrors were believed to be magical in and of themselves. Their reversal of reality even led them to be seen as evil in seventeenth-century Naples, and women were forbidden to keep them in the house. (And people call witches superstitious!) For the spellcrafter, that reversal of normal images may become part of a ritual seeking. Mirrors also serve as scrying tools and, being a little more mobile than bowls of water or forest pools, can be added to a portable altar.

NEEDLES/PINS: Despite their use in some voodoo rituals, needles and pins are more likely to be crafting tools for a magical practitioner. Silver or gold needles, reserved for use in preparing ritual garments, altar clothes, spell pouches, and bundles, are highly prized items, as they add elements of earth—or aspects of the masculine/feminine duality—to the items they complete.

PAPER: For collection into a *Book of Shadows* or as individual sheets for your notes on ritual, you'll want good-quality paper with archival qualities. You could make these sheets yourself, if you're familiar enough with paper ingredients to avoid any with high acid content that will severely limit the life of your pages. If you're not, consult a professional printer for your *Book of Shadows*. You'll want paper and bindings that are resilient but take your inks and pigments without soaking through.

Your knowledge of papermaking can, however, be turned to another use for spellcasting. When *Charmed*'s Phoebe cast a spell to heighten her intelligence ("The Painted World"), she wrote the spell on a small sheet of paper to provide a point of physical contact between her and the spell. Sympathetic magic, where one thing stands for, or symbolizes, another, is common in many workings. Piper and Phoebe's spell in "The Dream Sorcerer"—an attempt to find the perfect man from a written list of attributes—is another example of sympathetic magic. So, too, is their use of a slip of paper with "2-12-2009" written on it when, in "Morality Bites," the sisters need a concrete symbol of the ephemeral future they are trying to contact. For these uses, in which the paper is consumed in the spellcasting, you can make your own papers, taking the opportunity to add herbs or other ingredients that reflect your desire. Adding rose petals to the paper used to call a lover, for example, multiplies the efficacy of your spell by increasing the sympathetic sym-bolism that links the name on the paper with the lover you hope to find.

Envelopes of your own papers can replace pouches that hold items meant to be burned together or kept together for future use.

PENDULUM: If divination or dowsing will be part of your ritual work, using something to act as a pendulum is advisable. Of course, a personal item would work better than a generic one, but even among generic items, some pieces appear to work better than others. Since most people, places, and things are in touch with the ground at least part of the time, earth-based objects are often favored. Metals are good. A silver ring, an iron key, a gold locket that might hold the person or object's name on a piece of paper are all possibilities. A well-respected English witch uses her mother's tea ball! Crystals are often called in for this duty as well; clear ones are preferred over any specific color. Just such a crystal leads the Halliwells to their enemy in "That Old Black Magic." In any case, this object is one of the few that really should be kept apart for a singular purpose. Many witches wrap their pendulums in silk to avoid any unintentional handling.

PENS: After you've chosen ink and paper for your workings, don't neglect your pens as a source of inspiration and symbolism. Fountain pens can be convenient, especially if you make your own inks, but anything that can be dipped is a possibility. Wooden sticks of ash, rowan, willow, or elder; quills from birds; or even metal pins can bring something extra to your efforts.

RIBBONS: While the whole of a ritual should be a harmonious representation of the spellcaster's desire, a visual clue that these disparate elements have been brought together for a singular purpose is often the finishing touch to the physical preparations. In myriad colors that reflect the practitioner's will, ribbons can be used to physically link spell components, to bind practitioners to one another for a ritual working, or as a metaphor for the link a diviner wishes to establish with the person or object of his or her search. Whether ribbons are used to tie spell pouches closed, bind poppets, or gently confine a willing subject, the symbolism remains the same.

The binding spell from "That Old Black Magic," which makes use of a red ribbon, isn't the sort of spell found in books belonging to ethical practitioners, but one undertaken between two consenting spellcasters does indeed include a red ribbon as part of its symbolism.

SAGE: For banishing negative emotions, sage is traditionally cast on an open brazier, but it is no less effective if burned in a bunch, as Piper Halliwell did in "From Fear to Eternity."

SALT: Thrown over a shoulder into a devil's eye, bad luck if spilled, or good luck if sprinkled on the tongue, salt is one of the earliest spell components. Used since ancient times to cleanse crystals, it is still a part of most purification rituals. Cast as a circle, it protects against intrusion. As an ingredient in potions, it negates evil or negligent intentions. It was the last item added to Piper Halliwell's potion to undo a "joke spell" cast in "Animal Pragmatism."

SAND: Though sand could, obviously, represent the earth in a working, in purpose it is more akin to ink. Usually prepared in several colors, it is used to carefully mark the edges of protective circles, to create charms or hexes on a floor, or to draw runes and symbols the witch can use to visualize the different aspects of a ritual.

SILK: Silk, while a cloth and frequently used as a simple altar dressing, has more specific esoteric functions. Believed to be a sort of "psychic insulator," it is used to drape magical implements like balls, cauldrons, and braziers when they aren't in use. Tarot cards, rune stones, and other divinatory items are often kept in silk pouches. Amulets, talismans, and ritual robes often contain silk as well, to separate the objects or individuals from the physical world.

SOOT: One of the easiest of spell components to procure, soot is also one of the most useful. As a sort of "anti-chalk," it performs all of chalk's functions but with a negative connotation—which is not the same as evil. Where a chalk outline might define the edges of a doorway, an outline of soot prevents an area from becoming a doorway, keeping out dark elements and protecting the practitioner in yet another way.

As a substitute for black ink, soot can be imbued with extra properties, depending on its source material. Woods such as ash, oak, willow, and rowen are well known for their restorative or medicinal powers. Soot collected from the burning of those woods encompass the same qualities, with the added element of fire. As a solid form, like charcoal, or made into a liquid ink, soot can be used to form the written segments of many spells, though it isn't suitable for material in your *Book of Shadows*. It tends toward a higher acid content than would be appropriate for writing spells that you hope will last several lifetimes.

Perhaps because it is completely nonreflective, soot developed an association with shadows and things hidden from normal sight. One ritual suggests that a scrying ball covered in soot is a good starting point for divination work, the soot being gently blown from the surface as the search for a specific item is formed in the witch's mind. In the same manner, items covered in soot are believed to be safe from unwanted or intrusive attention. A cloth dusted in soot was believed to be a suitable protection for hiding other spell components or even grimoires. A symbolic smudge is still found on the covers of many a *Book of Shadows*.

A sprinkle of soot, considered a condensed form of smoke, can be an acceptable substitute for the burning of incense or candlelight when open fires might be unsafe. Dried herbs are often highly combustible; they can spark or even explode when exposed to heat. Mixing them with soot in a cold sachet maintains the balance of elements without endangering the witch's eyebrows. Preparing a good stock of soot from various woods or incenses will take time and effort, but provides a valuable and versatile addition to your pantry.

THREAD/CORD: Like ribbons, threads or cords are commonly used to unite the physical elements of a magical ritual, but they have several other purposes as well.

Colored threads, used in place of colored inks, can create runes or symbols on fabrics.

Cord, set in a circle, takes the place of other protective components such as salt.

While ribbons simply bind, thread indicates the practitioner's desire to fabricate a whole with a set pattern, which introduces a higher degree of order in the entire working.

WATER: Nearly half of all magical endeavors can benefit from the inclusion of water, whether spring, rain, blessed, or perfumed, in your ritual cabinet. For scrying, anointing, blessing, purifying, and divining, water is essential.

A Witch's Herb Garden

Planting these herbs provides a solid starting point for magical and medicinal preparations.

Agrimony	Angelica	Basil	Bay
Boneset	Broom	Burdock	Catnip
Chamomile	Chives	Cinquefoil	Coltsfoot
Fennel	Feverfew	Mint	Mugwort
Rue	Roses	Rosemary	Sage
Tansy	Thyme	Trefoil	Vervain
Valerian	Woodruff	Wormwood	Yarrow

Remembering that layers of meaning — compounded symbolism — can focus a witch's desires, consider planting your garden in a ritual pattern, or with plants grouped according to their esoteric functions, or in alignment with the cardinal quarters.

Before discarding the medievalist's belief in the magical and life-affirming powers of plants, consider this: After being given a lethal dose of strychnine under strict laboratory controls, a group of animals was immediately dosed with a preparation of bay oil. Every single animal survived! Science still doesn't know why.

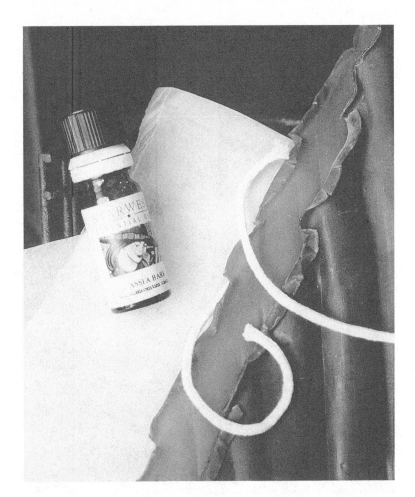

Essential oils, cotton wicks, and colored and plain beeswax are the basis for a versatile repertoire of candles. If you want to make your own, but don't want the heat or fuss of traditional candle making, you'll find oodles of options in your local craft store.

Candles

Ask most witches what one item they wouldn't be caught dead without and, invariably, it'll be candles. Rife with esoteric associations, candles also satisfy more basic, primitive needs for comfort, light, and hope.

Over the first two seasons of *Charmed*, hundreds of candles were used on the set. Fat ones, slender ones, dark ones, brilliant white tapers, and golden buttery beeswax candles have all adorned the attic altar. In this respect, art imitates life; all sorts of life. A conservative estimate of the number of candles dedicated

From divination to meditation to spellcasting, candles figure largely in most esoteric activities. Luckily, a varied selection won't break the bank, and even if you aren't thinking magical thoughts, they add a special beauty to any activity.

to religious use worldwide in a single year is over *eight billion*. The custom of burning candles crosses all cultural boundaries and all spiritual affiliations.

Like many other spell components, candles benefit from your personal touch. Making your own supply isn't a huge task and allows you to scent them with herbs and spices best suited to the rituals you regularly perform—or to create something truly special for a new rite.

Candle making is best undertaken in winter. You'll have time to dry or distill all the herbals that reach peak fragrance in the fall and you can take on the hot chore when it's cool outside. Medieval candle makers quickly discovered that plying their trade in the winter allowed them to stay cool and take advantage of the numerous natural molds they could make at once by pressing a broomstick—or maybe a wand—into the snow. Drop in a wick, pour your wax, wait just a few minutes for the snow to cool the wax, and you've got dozens of uniquely textured candles ready to store. And, as most spells call for the candles to burn out naturally, you know you're going to need a lot of them!

ꙮ A Candle Color Codex

White	Purification, transformation, divinity, blessings, peace (a moon symbol)
Black	Banishing, deflecting negativity, life changes
Red	Power, fire, vitality, life, lust, sexuality, physical energy, aggression (a sun symbol)
Silver	Peace, psychic energy, femininity, channeling, clairvoyance (a moon symbol)
Gold	Strength, prosperity, masculinity (a sun symbol)
Pink	Love, family, friendship
Green	Healing, health, fertility, luck, harmony
Blue	Protection, peace, truth (a water symbol)
Yellow	Balance, self-confidence, personal worth, friendship, creativity, communion, communication (an air symbol)
Orange	Abundance, prosperity, warmth
Purple	Judgment, wisdom, mysteries, learning, esoterica
Brown	Nature, animal, harmony, home (an earth symbol)
Natural	Balance, neutrality, harmony

CREATING AN HERBAL INCENSE

Fully half of the spells cast by the Halliwell sisters create smoke of one sort or another. For thousands of years, incense has served four basic functions: (1) to carry messages, (2) to heighten the practitioner's awareness of the ritual about to be performed, (3) to alter the spellcaster's perception, and (4) to purify spaces, implements, and people. Whether it is used to waft over oneself in spiritual cleansing or to peer through for visions, a witch's supply of incense needs to be regularly renewed.

Every incense contains a resin that encourages the other ingredients to burn well. Commercial resins are available, but many witches prefer frankincense for its sweet smoke and esoteric connotations.

Essential oils, in even minuscule amounts, play on the senses and, depending on the oils chosen, can help a witch relax and become receptive, or crank up the concentration for heavy visual workings. Because scent plays such a powerful role in our associative memories, oils are considered prime components in incenses used for scrying and divination.

Fresh and dried herbs and spices, used in full knowledge of their physical and metaphysical properties, bolster sympathetic magic rituals for the experienced practitioner.

Safety is always a factor when working with open or smoldering flames, and a significant portion of the practitioner's groundwork should be devoted to studying incense recipes to ensure that none are so combustible as to create a fire hazard; that any hallucinogenic properties are both anticipated and understood; and that none of the gases released are dangerous in confined spaces.

As most incense is burned over charcoal, you have yet another opportunity to work plant symbolism into your rite. Charcoal can be made from many species of tree, all of which have magical connotations. Rowan wood is associated with healing, both physical and emotional. Oak promotes strength and determination.

Apple wood, like its fruit and leaves, signifies love. Willow represents spiritual growth, while ash is associated with financial well-being.

QUARTZ

A silicate that arranges itself into rigid patterns while cooling from a molten form, quartz, in all its permutations of color and shape, is symbolic of both fire and earth, a combination difficult to obtain in such wide variety elsewhere.

The many colors and shapes of quartz each lend themselves to specific functions. Rose quartz focuses love, romance, friendship, fidelity, and peace, bringing happiness. Tourmulated quartz

Hanging from chandeliers, ears, necklaces, and hair, the Charmed Ones are surrounded by crystals of one sort or another. Where could you add a little crystal magic of your own?

allows far-seeing or, as some believe, true-seeing directed at people and events closer to hand. Clear quartz is associated with protection—remember all those ringing crystals on the chandelier that Leo would eventually be asked to repair in "Something Wicca This Way Comes"? Clear quartz for our favorite white lighter?—though, in larger pieces, it has been known to function as a scrying crystal.

Crystals, now used as magical objects, were once ground and eaten as medicines!

Agate: Stone of Many Colors

Red — Healing
Black — Success
Black and white — Defense against physical challenge
Blue — Respite from conflict
Earthy brown — Wealth
Mossy greens — Health
Striped — Physical strength and courage

A LITTLE CANDLE MAGIC, ANYONE?

Alyssa Milano isn't likely to pooh-pooh *all* the magic surrounding her on-screen character. After looking for love in all the wrong places, the actress discovered a shrink-wrapped love spell kit in a New Age bookshop and took it home. She lit and anointed the kit's candles, read the precomposed chant, and waited. In just a month, she'd met Cinjin Tate of Remy Zero. Less than a year later, the couple were happily married.

❧ A Partial List of the Charmed Candleworkings

EPISODE	USE/SPELL	QUANTITY	CANDLES
"Animal Pragmatism"	To make dates from animals	5	Red
"The Dream Sorcerer"	To find the man of your dreams	3	Blue
		2	White
		1	Red
		2	Black
"Feats of Clay"	Charm of confidence	4	Black
		2	White
	To increase confidence	4	Black
		2	White
"The Fourth Sister"	To summon Kali (full ritual)	5 (altar)	Black
		8 (floor)	Black
	To commune with Kali	4 (altar)	Black
"Morality Bites"	To move ahead in time	2	Blue
"She's a Man, Baby, a Man"	To attract a succubus	14	Blue
"Something Wicca This Way Comes"	To receive the Power of Three	9	White
	For protection and meditation (cast by another witch)	3	White
		2	Black
		3	Red
		1	Green
	To destroy Jeremy (the first demon the sisters faced)	9	White, anointed (including one birthday candle!)
"That '70s Episode"	To return the sisters to their own time	4	Black
"They're Everywhere"	To hear secret thoughts	2	Black

EPISODE	USE/SPELL	QUANTITY	CANDLES
"When Bad Warlocks Go Good"	To embrace a demon nature	11 (altar)	Black
	To draw a demon	2	Black
		1	Black atop an inverted cross
"The Witch Is Back"	To summon a deceased relative forward in time	4 (floor)	White
		3 (altar)	Black
		3 (altar)	White/ natural
	To send a deceased relative back in time	4 (floor)	Black
		3 (altar)	White/ natural
		3 (altar)	Black

The simplest altars are often the most evocative — don't crowd yourself unnecessarily.

The Witches' Place

A Place to Work

Spellcasting can happen just about anywhere. When Phoebe inadvertently turns all of P3's patrons into a petting zoo in "Animal Pragmatism," she hunkers down amid the ostriches and monkeys to whip up a reversal spell from scratch before her sisters can even get out of the parking lot! Clearly, a witch's work doesn't require a special space. Still, even the sisters, as well as most of the other practitioners they've encountered, have established a ritual space that they use whenever the option is available.

In "The Fourth Sister," Aviva's space is defined by a simple square of cloth and a collection of black candles. Portable and practical for someone living in temporary surroundings, her cloth provided her with an easily established altar, while her candles created a sacred circle within which she could work. You may find this elegantly simple solution fulfills all your needs as well, but if space and inclination allow, a more permanent or well-provisioned space may be more to your liking.

Since they have an attic bigger than many more modern apartments (not to mention hardwood floors and an east-facing window that must be hellish to replace when things go wrong), it's no wonder the Halliwell women established a permanent ritual space up there. Slightly more realistic options for real-world practitioners might be a small table, a deep window ledge or, for those with a garden, even an outdoor space. The key issues to consider as you search for your perfect place are safety first, followed in no particular priority by privacy, quiet, and purpose.

While security is necessary for concentration—no one can visualize a complicated staring pattern, for example, while worrying if he or she is about to be run over by a three-year-old on a tricycle—it's a practical consideration as well. Many workings will suggest the burning of candles or incense; others may lend themselves to heating scented oils. A spot too windy or drafty will extinguish your candles, while an outside location with dry leaves might inspire visitation from the local fire department instead of visions. Even inside, in apparently safe places, check for fabrics that could burn if a brazier or candle overturned. If you share your home with young children, remember that many items and materials used in spellcasting pose serious risks if mishandled or ingested.

So, your first order of business is to create a safe place for yourself and those around you. If absolutely nowhere suggests itself as appropriate, you may want to consider a box or chest that you can lock. The surface serves as altar and work space, the secure interior as storage for your tools. In addition to providing the necessary safety margin, a small chest is portable, a functional consideration for anyone, like a student, who tends to move often. A locked chest is also a prudent precaution for practitioners who,

Even if privacy isn't an issue for you, you may need extra security for your components if you live with, or invite, a lot of children to your home.

for whatever reason, and there are many, might want to keep their spellcasting completely private. Even within the fictional Halliwell household, where all the principals are fully aware and supportive of one another, Prue chooses the attic as her work space when she casts the spell to increase her powers in "Which Prue Is It Anyway?"

A good ritual space includes, in addition to safety, this measure of privacy. You will most likely keep not only your tools here, but your growing *Book of Shadows* as well. Like a diary, the book will likely contain your innermost thoughts, ideas for future workings, and notes on past rituals. A door that locks is an obvious aid to establishing privacy, but so too are freestanding screens, curtains, or the lock on your chest. Even timing can create solitude where none was obvious. Not every location is busy at all times. Your backyard, for example, may be full of squealing kids all day but a silent haven at night.

While privacy and quiet can be synonymous, they aren't always. My kitchen is incredibly private when dishes need washing, but it's hardly quiet. Your ideal work space should allow you the luxury of reading without earplugs, because you'll be doing a lot of it—and writing. Study is an intrinsic part of spell-casting and other ritual work. Just as familiarizing yourself with a new computer program is easier when you're sitting at your computer, spell practices are easier to consider when you can reach out and touch your tools. Quiet promotes focus, making each of your working sessions that much more productive. Again, if the physical surroundings of your work space don't seem conducive to peaceful contemplation, a simple adjustment in your own timing may put you in the right place at the most quiet time of day. *Plan* your sessions ahead of time. Have all the materials you intend to study and all the necessary tools ready, and, most important, be in the right mindset *before* entering your space. Come prepared to work and, even if you don't find absolute silence, you'll be better able to block out daily distractions. Over time, merely entering your space will help you focus on your plans and desires.

Ultimately, those plans and desires will determine where you work. Each practitioner brings specific emotional and spiritual concerns to a working. The Halliwell attic, in addition to being safe, private, and quiet, provides a physical link to previous generations of Halliwell women. We learn in "That '70s Episode" that both the sisters' mother and grandmother used the attic as their ritual space. Real-world spaces will have particular associations for you as well. You may not have generations of witches to whom you'd like to make an emotional connection, but you may have a special space where you retreated with a good book as a child, or a favorite haunt where you and your best friend exchanged secrets. Or perhaps you're seeking an even greater sense of connection, and you find yourself closest to that when in a woodland space you've never seen before. If so, that portable chest we discussed earlier might well be a backpack! Even if you establish a single permanent work space, the purpose of your working may feel better if carried out elsewhere.

Whenever possible, your work space should reflect your personality, dreams, and hopes. Including nonmagical items that inspire you is perfectly acceptable — even desirable.

Practicalities such as the amount of space available may force you to move to a temporary location elsewhere. Imagine trying to arrange all the ritual elements taken up by the gender-switching spell in "She's a Man, Baby, a Man!" in a closet work space! If your rituals tend to sprawl, you'll need to keep that in mind when choosing your space. In "Witch Trial," the sisters abandon their attic in favor of an outdoor site where other witches have gathered before. The basis of every spell and every working is purpose. Don't forget that the place can reflect that purpose as effectively as your ritual or components.

The Tools of Magic

Once you've found the ritual space that works best for you, you'll want to furnish it with all the components you've diligently studied and collected as well as the other, nonconsumable items that help aim your desire. From the very first episode, "Something Wicca This Way Comes," *Charmed* has gently balanced its adherence to actual Wiccan practices with the necessity of props and plots. Andy Trudeau's explanation of an athema, "...it's a ceremonial tool. Witches use them to direct energy...," is textbook. As you've undoubtedly noticed, tools, even in *Charmed*, vary with the practitioner. One witch's altar may overflow, while another's seems spartan. Choosing the tools most appropriate to your purposes and workings will eventually lead to your own equally unique collection.

Just as chess players often chuckle at the scenarios set up on movie or television chess boards—situations no sensible players would ever find themselves in—altars set up by prop people are frequently assembled for appearance, not function. For those with a dedicated altar, unlimited space, and an abundance of tools, keeping everything out and in the open may be an option, but as each working is designed to address a particular purpose, filling your work space with everything you own is more likely to contribute to mental and physical clutter. Most practitioners dress their work space from the bottom up—from altar cloth to lighting—for each ritual, showing a discriminating eye and hand in choosing implements to complement their intentions.

Choosing the items you'll include inside your work space for each new ritual is the first step toward organizing a new spell. Witches aren't stage magicians; they don't have to bring out all the tricks at once.

THE MAJOR TOOLS

ALTAR: A flat stone, a window ledge, a wall shelf, a cloth spread on the ground, a chalked outline on the floor—almost anything can be the focus of your ritual space as long as it is stable enough to let you work without worrying about candles tipping, and smooth enough not to catch or tangle fingers or sleeves. Beyond providing a flat, stable surface, your choice of altar will usually reflect some aspect of your philosophy and aesthetic. Wiccans with strong tendencies toward natural motifs in their magic may opt for an altar of a particular wood. Others may prefer stone slabs. Most, however, will use a table of some sort, usually one that can serve more than one purpose if space is tight.

The usual working altar on *Charmed*, a low table around which the sisters can sit comfortably on the floor, is an excellent model if you have enough square footage. Small enough that everyone can reach the entire surface, but large enough to accommodate all the tools you might need, is the ideal. Naturally, solo practitioners will require a smaller surface than a group. For practitioners who like to incorporate reflections of all four elements, a low table can serve as a connection to earth. Similarly, a tall table like Zoe's, seen in "From Fear to Eternity," represents air.

ALTAR CLOTH: The very first thing acquired for most work areas is an altar cloth. Whether elaborate or plain, the cloth marks the space for ritual use. For those whose altars must also serve as desks or coffee tables, the cloth is a physical reminder that, during the working at least, this is a sacred place. It may revert to the same stretch of wood over which you and your kids argue the relative merits of homework, but while that cloth covers it, it is holy ground. An altar cloth obviously isn't just a table dressing and deserves some thought on the practitioner's part.

As color plays an important role in keying the witch's mind to her purpose, a collection of cloths in various shades isn't unusual. Embellishment of a single cloth can serve the same purpose. A ring of symbols meaningful to the practitioner can be embroidered, or otherwise worked, around the edge of the cloth and can be draped over the working space to bring a single symbol to the front.

While the material itself isn't particularly important, you'll only have to chase that pretty piece of slippery black satin a few times before realizing that whatever beauty it might bring to your ritual is more than countered by its inconvenience. And, while Scotchgard isn't something you'll want to add to your altar cloths, washable fabrics that easily release the odd spill of ash, wax, or oil will make your experience more pleasurable.

CAULDRON: Often the centerpiece of a ritual working, the cauldron evokes the element of water, though it is as often filled with sand! Generally an iron or earthen pot on three legs, the cauldron remains a working implement for holding spell components—though no longer for boiling, grinding, or cooking them. Other tools serve those purposes.

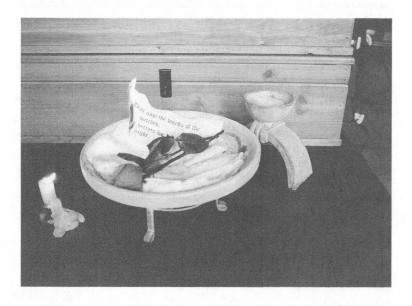

Even if you regularly practice indoors, you can bring something seasonal to your workings. A cauldron of sand in summer and snow in winter is a simple reminder of the turning of time and the connections between the practitioner and the environment in which they work.

In "Something Wicca This Way Comes," Piper's rose-pierced poppet gets tucked into the cauldron that sits in the Halliwells' work space. When Phoebe burns the spell components to draw Melinda Warren to the future in "The Witch Is Back," and in "Morality Bites," when paper containing the future year they visit is burned, everything goes into the cauldron. Filled with sand or snow, the cauldron is a safe repository for hot workings. In fact, the word "cauldron" comes from two words, one of which is "hot." The other, not surprisingly, is "boil." Filled with water, the cauldron accepts tokens and items that are ritually hidden during a working. Aromatic oils or perfumed waters gently warmed in the cauldron release their scents slowly and recall the element of air. Often associated with the female aspect of knowledge, a cauldron is visualized as a vessel from which life, spiritual or magical, flows.

Prepared incenses come in wonderful varieties. Experiment with some of them outside of ritual so you'll know what sensory input to add to your workings. You'll soon find yourself combining and adjusting as you develop favorites.

CENSER: Though the cauldron can accept most flammable spell items, the censer is reserved for burning one important spell component: incense. Censers come in two basic types, brazier and open. A brazier holds a base layer of charcoal, over which loose incense can be sprinkled, and will produce more copious smoke than an open censer. A ventilated cover is common on brazier-styled censers, especially if you happen to find a Far Eastern design. The thuribles commonly used to cense the altars and celebrants during Roman Catholic and Episcopalian services are brazier censers, though these, intended to be swung about during the service, are hung from long chains or cords. The incense used inside them is most likely to be flaked, dusty, or some loose form.

Open censers, on the other hand, are used primarily for incense sticks and blocks. Often little more than a weight with an opening into which a stick can be inserted, this form of censer takes up very little space. Equally simple in form is the open plate designed for blocks or cones. Your censer choice will be based on the incense you prefer, but if your ritual clothing includes loose folds or long sleeves, keep that in mind when furnishing your altar, and pick a heavy design that completely encloses any burning material or flame.

ATHAME: Andy Trudeau knows his athames from his filleting knives and, while the Halliwell sisters have yet to make use of this traditional tool, their existence in the *Charmed* universe reflects broad usage in the real world of Wiccan practice.

Though design varies from a short knife no longer than the hand to a short sword length, the blade is most often blunt and

The athames most often seen on modern altars are short, but they're not the only possibility. Arm-length blades are not only acceptable but practical if you're six feet tall and need to cast a circle on the floor. Your tools should fit you and be comfortable in your hand.

double-edged. The blind, or unsharpened, edges don't interfere with the tool's functionality; it was never meant to cut anything, merely to give direction to the energy raised by the witch. Perhaps its most common use is in casting a working circle, a protective first step in many rituals. One version of a casting that specifically requires an athame is the Triple Circle. The first circle is cast in chalk, the second in salt, the last traced through the first two with the athame. This symbolic definition, cleansing, and direction make any space suitable for further rituals or castings.

Just as the cauldron is often linked with femininity, the athame provides elements of masculinity. It's also associated with air and is often used to trace symbols in that element. Because of its role as an energy conduit, some traditions prefer to connect it to fire.

BOLLINE: While the blunt athame serves its function perfectly, a knife that actually cuts something is also a customary implement for an altar. Unlike the athame, the bolline is kept well sharpened—not that easy to do, as the sickle-shaped blade is often made of silver or copper, softer metals that aren't anxious to hold an edge. Still, the knife is practical: Used to gather herbs in season, trim wicks on lamps and candles, and etch symbols in candles, among other things, it's the one tool that is used as often away from the ritual space as inside it. Some Wiccans keep two bollines, one for use inside the space and another for outside formal ritual. The handles of both athames and bollines may give some hint to their usual usage. The athame, used solely within a sacred space, features a black handle. Bollines used inside the circle are also black-handled, while those used outside its confines are generally white. Either blade may be inscribed with runes, symbols, or the practitioner's name.

Some ascribe the bolline to druidic tradition. Certainly its shape, reminiscent of the tiny scythes with which the druids were reputed to harvest mistletoe from oaks, is quite similar.

The only sharp implement used in the work space in the Halliwell attic was used to prick the fingers of all three sisters in preparation for bringing Melinda Warren out of the past, but that knife was, in all probability, one of those filleting knives with which aspiring chefs, such as Piper, like to stock their kitchens.

WAND: Though only one wand has made an appearance in the *Charmed* universe—a wand that couldn't even be used by a witch!—wands of various types are common Wicca implements which may very well pop up in future episodes. A wand remains the one implement many witches consider essential to their ritual work.

Just as the cauldron is associated with the feminine aspects of knowledge, the wand represents the masculine aspects. Considered a phallic symbol for obvious reasons, its purpose is similar to the athame, the direction of energy and will. Unlike the athame, whose influence is usually seen as directed only within the work space, a wand's area of affect is considerably more global. Rituals affecting large groups of people, or large areas of land, frequently employ a wand instead of an athame.

The physical appearance of a wand follows no set guidelines. In parts of Wales, wands are equated with staffs and can be up to seven or eight feet long. In Germany, broom handles might also be wands. For modern Wiccans, however, the wand is a much shorter length of wood (other materials turn up, but rarely) that fits easily in the hand. One wand per practitioner is another rule of thumb, although, as with most things symbolic, this isn't true of all witches. A smaller percentage prepares wands for specific purposes and may own nine or more, combining different woods, colors, crystals, and runes for a singular desire, such as healing.

Wands are highly personal items. Covered in knotted string, decorated with crystals, incised with names or symbols, each reflects the practitioner's primary spiritual goals. It may take an entire lifetime to create a wand. In fact, one Welsh poem tells of a young woman's growing the tree for her wand's wood. As the wood used was deadfall, meaning that it fell from the tree rather than being taken by force, the girl was quite old before she even began the wand! You likely won't have that much patience—or even live in the same place long enough to attempt such a feat—but, as your wand may well be the only one you ever use, give it considerable thought before beginning.

BROOM: Hardly reserved for modern Wiccan usage, the broom's long association with magical ritual has, rather unfortunately, been "mythconception." It is most often pictured as some magical conveyance by which witches might flit about the countryside at the full of the moon, instead of a tool used in ritual purification of a working space.

Also known as the besom, this particular broomstick isn't intended to leave your ritual space. Whether full-sized or, as is more often the case, scaled down to the size of a typical whisk, it is meant to clear the altar and its environs of unwanted or negative energy prior to a working; or to help close down the work space after a ritual, to leave no residuals that might interfere with

Hardly practical for sweeping out the kitchen, is it? The symbolic nature of this Welsh example of a besom is fairly obvious. Because it is made fresh for every rite, it becomes an opportunity to bring additional layers of meaning to your working.

THE WORKING ELEMENT

A Personal Growth Exercise

The broom has a longer historical link to spellcasting than most other ritual tools, including a belief that it was once used for real, physical travel. Modern times have suggested that this travel might refer to "astral travel," or an out-of-body experience.

Does this imagery reinforce or contradict its more common purpose as outlined here?

_____

_____

How might this imagery be incorporated into ritual?

_____

_____

later spellcasting. Ash or birch are the traditional woods for a broom; you may find others more appropriate to your desires. A hand-carved broom is difficult to find nowadays, but, with care and patience, you can make your own.

On an elemental level, a broom is a tool of air. Possessing both a shaft which, like the wand, is often associated with phallic symbolism, and a brush—seen as feminine—a besom is often considered the joining of male and female aspects, therefore sexually neutral or sexually perfected, depending on your own viewpoint.

CHALICE: This tool, a stemmed cup, does precisely what it appears to do: It holds infusions and tonics, libations of all sorts, drunk to promote health or visions or to honor the earth or the creator. Do make sure, therefore, that, regardless of its appearance, your chalice is made of nontoxic materials—no pewter or lead-based enamels as ornamentation. Numerous beautiful old cups can fulfill this role, but be positive that the components meet _modern_ standards for contact with foods.

Hand-thrown from local clay, wrapped in silver, or simple glass made beautiful for having been a gift, each of these chalices brings something different to the spells for which they're used.

Like the cauldron, the chalice is a vessel of health and vision, a feminine component in magical ritual, and, in any number of traditions and mythologies, a source of life, whether actual or spiritual. Its use in ritual is an affirmation of life, a plea for fertility, a thanks for health. Not surprisingly, it brings the element of water and its symbolism to a working.

THE MINOR TOOLS

Who wouldn't love to see this fellow smiling at you as you began a spell? If your magic doesn't bring some joy to your life, you're going about it all wrong!

CANDLE HOLDER: The altar that doesn't include candles is a rarity indeed; a well-equipped space will include a variety of holders. Some reflect the witch's particular tradition. This one (*see left*) harkens back to the druidic elements incorporated into modern Wiccan tradition. Other holders are chosen specifically for their metal or crystal properties. Silver, representative of the hidden, the metaphysical, and the unknown, remains popular, as does simple iron as a stand-in for the earth element. Wooden holders add a natural aspect to a working and, like altar woods, can hold several meanings.

MORTAR AND PESTLE: The mortar and pestle, still the symbols of modern pharmacology, harken back to a time long before Wicca was established, and links all the esoteric arts—even if they are now quantified and deemed sciences. Alchemists, herbalists, witches, and scientists have treasured these practical tools; you will as well.

On a purely symbolic level, the mortar and pestle, like the besom, represent sexual completion, the unity of male and female influences, a balance. The mortar, like most cup- or bowl-shaped objects is seen as female, a vessel. The pestle, a phallic symbol, is by itself a tool of destruction but, in combination with the mortar, is an instrument of creation.

More practically, mortar and pestle represent the healing functions long associated with arcane pursuits. In this light, you may find good use for these tools. Many herbs and other plants release their oils only when bruised. Other natural components, especially grains or seeds, must be ground before their scents can be appreciated. The preparation of incense is greatly enhanced with these simple tools.

There are wooden mortars and pestles but, unless you have several and are prepared to keep them well marked, you'll likely find that scents and tastes carry over from one working to the next, which may cause unintended—and unpleasant—combinations. A pharmacological set is the answer. The smooth, hard surfaces release residual grit, tastes, and smells easily.

A variety of mortar and pestle sets have appeared in *Charmed*. During the very last moments of the confrontation in "That '70s Episode," all the components for the Nicholas-Must-Die spell end up in a mortar and pestle instead of the usual receptacle, the cauldron. In that episode, the mortar and pestle were used in the final compilation of spell ingredients, which was handled in less than a second! A more usual application, the preparation of a potion for a future working, occurs in "The Devil's Music" when Phoebe grinds together the ingredients for a demonic enema. Different mortar and pestle sets were used for each blending.

BELL: Bells aren't the private reserve of church steeples, though those are one example of this common arcane tool. Just as smoke is believed to carry messages, prayers, and hopes to a higher authority or level of self-awareness, certain sounds have traditionally been believed to cleanse the air through which their reverberations pass, carrying good wishes. Firecrackers in the east, cowbells to ward off the evil eye in European mountains, even shotgun blasts at midnight on New Year's Eve were all originally intended to purify and clear away evil thoughts or intentions. "By bell, book and candle," begins one version of a Christian exorcism rite.

Bells and chimes, a musical first cousin, can be thought of as auditory smoke. In an invocation where incense was inappropriate, the single peal of a ritual bell might provide the perfect alternative. A lovely outside meditation, The Wind Sculptor, requires that several sets of light chimes be hung among a grouping of trees to familiarize the magical practitioner with the interaction of wind and leaves. With practice, a witch can anticipate how a breeze will move through a particular tree by noting the order in which the chimes are stroked by the wind. Some claim that, with sufficient understanding, one can not only predict the wind's path but gently nudge it on this very localized scale.

Not all bowls are looked *into*; some, like this one, are meant to be looked *through*. Don't be afraid to experiment with the traditional tools until you find one that works best for you.

BOWL: Though some practitioners will use their cauldrons or a chalice for divination, many others prefer to use a special bowl. Unlike the multipurpose cauldron, the scrying bowl is dedicated to this single task and, between uses, is often wrapped in silk to buffer it from random thoughts. In general, the bowl's interior surface will be either dark or highly polished and filled with some fluid medium just before use. Water is typical but by no means the only choice. Ink, oils, even teas find their way into scrying bowls. In keeping with the psychic isolation suggested by the silk wrappings, the water, ink, or oils are removed at the end of the session and will not be reused.

OIL BURNER: Some witches use oils only on their candles or their persons and never need specific tools for burning or warming oils. Yet oils often are warmed gently in an oil burner to release the scents that focus practitioners on the task at hand or allow their awareness to float freely. Perhaps you prefer greater control of how much scent is released or your combination of oils. Oil burners include a shallow bowl to hold the oil and a firm support that holds a candle beneath the bowl. Almost any witch could craft an efficient oil burner, but if time or inclination doesn't allow, various styles with assorted capacities are commercially available.

Many of your tools can be decorative as well as functional. Like the little cherubs, which carry messages, the scents from warmed oils can act as spiritual messengers, carrying hopes and dreams.

THE DIVINATORY TOOLS

Divination, though usually associated with predicting the future, is actually a process, a ritual, designed to bring something misplaced or hidden into the open in a present time. Recovering information lost in time, or finding something or someone hidden in the present, are as much a part of divination as anticipating upcoming events.

As divination, in this wider interpretation, is one of the most often attempted rituals practiced on *Charmed*, it seems appropriate to investigate the specialized ritual tools associated with divination a little more closely.

Most divination tools are well established, with keys to aid interpretation. The Tarot, the I Ching, and the rune stones, while not specifically tools of witchcraft, can nonetheless provide guidance and alternatives.

CRYSTAL BALL: Often jokingly referred to as the domain of sideshow mystics, the use of a crystal ball of some type for divination goes back at least forty-five hundred years in Mongolia, Turkey, Ethiopia, and dozens of other locations. Originally, lumps of raw native crystal were the medium of choice. The first polished crystals date to about 400 B.C., but, as polishing crystals was much harder than shaping balls of glass—once glassblowing itself was mastered—glass balls later became popular choices as well. A few of the rarer type of glass balls, those filled with unmixable colored oils or equal parts of water and a colored oil, can still be found, but these fragile antique constructs command high prices. Much more available and reasonably priced are the so-called witch-balls, balls of silvered glass, usually with an unusual coruscating color cast over their surfaces. For the truly economy-minded, there's even a theory that modern snow globes and lava lamps refer to this most common of divination tools.

The primary method of crystal divination, with the ball substituting for a scrying bowl or mirror, is self-evident. Or is it?

The most oft-heard comment from the patron sitting opposite the sideshow mystic is, of course, "Hey, I can't see anything down in there." And he or she can't. Contrary to the patron's belief, the practitioner of crystal divination wasn't seeing anything *in* the ball either, and certainly not *down* in the ball.

Contemporary hypnotists might encourage their subjects to focus on a swinging object held just above the normal line of sight. Religious mystics of a variety of faiths tend to adopt the same posture during their meditations, sitting or kneeling, usually on the floor, with their gaze fixed on a candle or other object, once again slightly above the immediate line of sight. In the original form of crystal divination, the crystal became the focus object, with the gazer seated on the floor looking *up* into a ball or unworked crystal. One of the most famous of crystal balls, the Curraghmore

Arranged for viewing in the modern fashion, either on a table stand or in the hand, these balls can also be suspended when removed from their silk-lined storage containers. Simply set them on a window ledge or mantelpiece. Try it — see if they change more than your perspective!

t h e   w i t c h e s '   p l a c e

Crystal, which was "liberated" from the Holy Lands by Godefroy de Bouillon in the twelfth century, is surrounded by a silver ring and was always hung from a set of chains (just above the normal sight line for a seated individual), and was never placed on a stand, as most modern balls are, or held in the hand.

Light playing on its surface, or the interior motions of fluid-filled glass balls, created patterns similar to those found in candle flames and, like the twirling watch, allowed conscious thought to be pushed gently to one side while unconscious perceptions, even perhaps *outside* perceptions, rose to the forefront for contemplation. Learning to direct that thought flow, while maintaining the free-floating mental state where inspiration is most fertile, is the heart of divination, the much-maligned crystal ball is a valuable tool in learning this vital skill.

Crystal's secondary use in divination is considerably more active and makes for much better TV than having three women simply stare into a ball for long periods of screen time. Crystal-dowsing, a related skill, is showcased in episodes like "That Old Black Magic."

Though, strictly speaking, almost any item of the right weight could function as a dowsing object to hold over a map, crystal, with all its meditative and divinatory connotations, is the one that opens the mental gate for many. The purpose of the crystal, in addition to acting as a pointer over maps or photos, is to allow the scryer to focus conscious thought on the reflections and refractions of light in the swinging pendulum. Time spent before a regular crystal ball pays off in an almost automatic triggering of those deeper mental reactions. Once the conscious concerns and questions are put in a secondary position, dozens of tidbits of knowledge can bump freely against one another until insight sharpens to certainty and the pendulum points to a site suggested by a very different sort of logic.

Needless to say, either use of your crystal will require concerted practice. After all, few of us know someone "lucky" enough to locate the lost or stolen as easily as Phoebe and Piper find Prue when they use Maggie Murphy as a living pendulum in "Murphy's Luck."

SPIRIT BOARDS: Like crystal balls, spirit boards, which are often sold alongside Monopoly and Scrabble games, have fallen into recent disrepute. Even *Charmed*'s Halliwell sisters, who supposedly grew up in a house where magical subjects weren't completely unknown, think of their spirit board as a parlor game—a game at which Phoebe often "cheats" by pushing the pointer!

At what time in history the spirit board, often called the ouija board, became a tool for telekinetic spirits instead of a human medium's implement is unclear; but in its original use, all parties present at the spirit board divination would have *expected* the medium to push the pointer!

If you've ever awakened from an incredible dream that you felt compelled to share, and noted with dismay how very quickly those vivid images can fade, or found yourself in mid-recollection suddenly unsure of exactly what *did* happen at the end, you'll understand how difficult it can be to translate dream or visionary images into specific words. Yet that is exactly what is asked of the medium behind the spirit board. Small wonder some mnemonic aid was developed to help cross that communication gap.

Traditional spirit board users worked in pairs. One acted as the medium, the other as a sort of secretary, noting the questions being asked of the medium and the responses indicated on the board. Only after the session was complete would the pair fill in the blanks in this spiritualistic shorthand. For example, if asked "Where is my grandfather's will?," the medium might point to a "D" and continue with the next question without interrupting the meditative state. After the session, the secretary would repeat the question and say, "You pointed to *D* at that time, why?" The medium would then explain the missing imagery or symbolism: "I saw it in a drawer." Or perhaps a particular scene is recalled by

Even the Parker Brothers version of a spirit board may add to your workings if you can find a partner who understands its intended use.

that letter which the medium, using the clue, can know separate from whatever other images presented themselves.

While speech is undoubtedly our primary means of communication, the act of vocalization *isn't* the best means of conveying mental images. Psychiatric patients are often instructed to keep a dream journal and to write down what they've dreamed immediately upon waking. Patients who've tried to use a tape recorder instead discover that fewer details are captured this way and that their spoken descriptions quickly degenerate from full sentences to lists of single words. The link between mind and hand seems much more natural than the link between mind and tongue.

A spirit board is a useful tool for practitioners who have working partners, if both parties understand the process and aren't sitting about waiting for disincarnate beings just seeking someone to provide a pointer for them to push about. As with crystal balls and other divinatory tools, the onus remains on the practitioner to find a meditative state where creativity and intuition can work well enough to provide the medium with something to communicate in the first place—which means Phoebe was probably doing it just right all along!

THE WORKING ELEMENT

A Personal Growth Exercise

The pointer on a modern ouija board is usually called the planchette, but planchettes had other, earlier, uses of their own. The hole through which we now read letters and numbers was once designed to hold a pencil, charcoal, or piece of chalk. The medium held the planchette and used it to write and draw across a large piece of paper or a table top. This early form of automatic writing is clearly related to the use of a spirit board. How might this variation be better suited to a solitary practitioner?

_____

_____

In all likelihood, you won't be rushing out to purchase all these items at once. In fact, it's probably better to acquire each of the items that seems to fit your practice one at a time. Think of your work space as a set of balances. Each tool you bring to it will have to mesh smoothly with those you have now or plan to find later. An altar of nothing but silver tools might be attractive, satisfy one aesthetic desire, and be completely appropriate to some types of divination, but it also may come up short if the work you intend to do affects, for example, a physical environment traditionally symbolized by wooden or clay items, or perhaps healing with the associated stone and crystal tools of these arts.

Along the way, you'll have to determine how you'll care for each item. Tarot cards, crystals, mirrors, almost any divination tools, in fact, are often wrapped in silk to insulate against unwanted metaphysical influences. Wooden tools may need to be oiled regularly. Metals can tarnish if not properly stored. Time spent caring for your magical tools, like any others, pays for itself in longer life and a firmer "feel" for how they can be better used.

✺ THE WORKING ELEMENT

A Personal Growth Exercise

The casting of the Triple Circle normally requires the use of three items: chalk, salt, and an athame. How might a bell be substituted into this protective ritual?

Dressing for the Occasion—Or Not

Last but not least are the items that you, as the practitioner, choose to wear while you prepare your rituals and invocations. In "Witch Trials," Piper is introduced to, and initially embarrassed by, one option for magical working—nudity. There are others. All have their own significance, and again, individual practitioners may find some arguments more persuasive than others.

The first option is to treat the clothing for your ritual work as you would the tools you use and the components you incorporate; that is, treat each working as a unique operation and choose this last tool, your clothing, as carefully and individually as you have the other elements. Some witches use the color of their clothing as a mental key to help focus on a particular working: For example, green robes for healing, blue for meditation, or red to draw a lover.

Other practitioners have a single garment for all their workings. Donning this robe or overcloak is the trigger for entering a meditative state from which all other rituals are taken. This robe may be differentiated for various workings by the color of a cord drawn around the waist or other visible symbolism.

If a singular garment is chosen for all operations, it is most likely to be black—not to be associated in any way with so-called black magic. Magical practice is, if nothing else, democratic. Every path is individual, so no witch can truly be said to be higher or lower than another. The use of unadorned black robes

Seasonal symbolism helps remind a witch, especially an urban witch, of the turning of the season, perhaps suggesting ritual work that should be undertaken during specific months, seasons, or phases of the moon, or simply recalling the connections between witch and world.

symbolizes both the commonality of the search for knowledge and empowerment, and the equality of the seekers.

For some, black is also symbolic of their avocation. Because the witch's day runs from noon of one day to noon of the next—beginning and ending in the light, with the night set aside for efforts outside the common tasks of the day—a night-dark robe also reflects that the tasks undertaken while wearing it are separate and apart from everyday practice, even in daylight.

Still others feel that their magical and spiritual endeavors *are* an intrinsic part of their daily lives, a part that should be more

the witches' place

The pointed hat most often associated with a witch's ritual clothing was actually an invention of the Christian Church, which hoped that placing a "steeple-crowned" hat on a heretic or a witch would attract God's notice and bring redemption for their souls.

connected with the physical world around them, not less so. These are the witches most likely to practice "skyclad" or "starclad," without any clothing at all. For them, this choice opens up a new way to experience the world around them, to return to an innocence and open-mindedness they may not have otherwise felt. Within a group ritual, nudity re-creates all members in equality, putting aside trappings of class or rank.

In any case, a choice of garment—or lack thereof—is no more ironclad than any of the other choices you will make as you compose your rituals. You may approach one working in one set of clothes, another with none, yet another in the middle ground many practitioners choose; clad but barefoot.

The important point is to give yourself the benefit of an informed choice. Even among the fictitious Halliwell clan, there is room for individualism. Between "That '70s Episode" and "Witch Trial," we've seen these wise women choose everything from the nudity Phoebe (and eventually even Piper) embraces within a single group working, to Patty Halliwell's use of ritual garments

A quick note on incense. It's designed to *smolder*, not burn with an open flame. After lighting an incense stick, cone, or block, blow out the flame and let it burn slowly.

for workings only, to Grams's choice—which, from the little we've seen of her, appears to be a case of adapting her ritual garments for everyday use—to the Charmed Ones' usual choice to bring everyday garments to ritual work.

THE SACRED WOODS

Since the Wiccan ideal often incorporates a respect for nature as one of its unwritten rules, many ritual tools are handmade of natural materials like wood. Not all woods are created equal, however, and many have established associations which can enhance the implements of knowledgeable practitioners.

Oak, historically tied to druidic practices, is perhaps the wood most frequently thought of in magical terms; but Wiccan precepts encompass nine sacred trees or woods, which also include apple, birch, elder, fir, hawthorn, hazel, rowan, vine, and willow. References to these woods appear in several long variations of the Wiccan Rede as well as in esoteric poetry like this anonymous piece:

Of the Woods

Nine woods in the Cauldron go,
Burn them fast and burn them slow.

Birch in the fire goes,
To represent what the Lady knows.

Oak gives the forest towers might,
In the fire brings the God's insight.

Rowan is the tree of power,
Causing life and magic to flower.

Willows at the waterside stand,
To aid the journey to the Summerland.

As Phoebe and Piper discovered, witches who celebrate outdoors often prefer to work their rites skyclad.

Hawthorn is burned to purify,
And draw faerie to your eye.

Hazel, the tree of wisdom and learning,
Adds its strength to the bright fire burning.

White are the flowers of Apple tree,
That brings us fruits of fertility.

Grapes that grow upon the vine,
Giving us both joy and wine.

Fir does mark the evergreen,
To represent immortality unseen.

Elder is the Lady's tree,
Burn it not or cursed you'll be.

Knowledge of these associations allow adepts to create tools specific to their desire, to create altars and other work spaces that better reflect their will, and to produce more individual brazier smoke.

A Time for Spells

Not surprisingly, spellcasting is often compared to cooking: Take these ingredients, put in this tool, mix with that tool, follow the directions, and hope for the best. If you look at only the visible elements of magical workings, the simile isn't bad. Unfortunately, what's left out of that description is more important than what's left in. It ignores the individual nature of each working, the multitude of tiny choices that ultimately shape the experience to the practitioner's desire. If it really were that simple, everyone could work minor miracles on a daily basis.

Of course, as you'll have gathered by now—supposing you didn't skip the last three chapters to get to the "good stuff" in this one—is that spellcasting isn't simple at all.

Up until now, we've been collecting not only items and ingredients, but knowledge. Little bits and pieces, to be sure, but scraps that, finally, are beginning to come together as you contemplate the ritual uses to which you'll soon be putting them. Just as the Halliwell sisters were once bound only to those spells and workings that were already written in their *Book of Shadows*, you too might easily have seen the spells outlined in this chapter as immutable recipes. They aren't. They are guides, examples to which you will bring the knowledge acquired in the earlier chapters, and from which you'll devise rituals that speak to your own personal imagery. The ritualistic progress of the Halliwell sisters, while completely fictional, does illustrate an important caution, however—crawl before you walk, walk before you run. Naturally, you'll want to move quickly from simply reading spells to adapting spells and on to creating your own new rituals, but, as Phoebe illustrates in "Animal Pragmatism," when she fills P3 with a veritable zoo of animals, a little forethought can prevent a lot of disaster control after the fact!

Adepts might spend weeks devising new rituals—and then wait even longer to carry them out if the symbolism of a particular time or season seems more appropriate to a working. Healing spells, for example, are often begun under a new moon, as it is believed that extra energy is available to some witches at that time. Even when you think you've considered every aspect of your new spell, you'll likely benefit from putting it aside for a short time so you can come back to it fresh and give it a second look. You'll be surprised at how much more you'll be able to refine your workings after some sober thought.

Though television's hectic pace simply can't accommodate the time required to broadcast a complete ritual working every episode or so, thereby revealing the full complexity of most magical efforts, real rituals, though individual, do follow a general, recognizable pattern. You may find this guide to the elements of any ritual helpful in preparing your own workings.

1. *Preparation of self:* This concept may seem self-evident, but as the composer of the ritual, you are the most important element in the working. You may have created the most integrated of magical plans, but unless you are ready, physically, mentally, and spiritually, to carry out that plan, the ritual is just a recipe. To prepare themselves for this most unusual activity, many practitioners spend the first moments of the ritual stepping back a pace to clear their thoughts and reexamine their motives. If, for any reason, you aren't completely comfortable with what you're about to undertake, stop. For many witches, this last bit of soul-searching takes place during a ritual bath, the discarding of everyday clothes, and the donning of ritual garb. Others do it during a period of fasting and meditation, yet others while anointing their skin or hair with scented oils or water. By the time they're ready to move on to the second step, they are already centered and confident.

2. *Preparation of the space:* This step often encompasses two separate, but related, actions—the sealing of the circle, followed by cleansing and warding the space and people inside the circle. Depending on the degree of preparation, the cleansing can be as simple as a short, spoken statement of intention or as complex as the casting of a Triple Circle, the exorcism of any residual energies from previous workings, the cleansing of all the tools to be used in the workings, and several spells of both personal and general protection. Some practitioners follow these steps with the invocation of particular spiritual authorities, others with a restatement of their purpose and intent. In either case, the specific working will begin only after these preliminary steps have been completed.

3. *Dressing the space:* The first step of any ritual is to assemble the necessary items within the protected space. Altars will be

dressed now. All the carefully chosen components (even if they consist of nothing more than a single candle held in the hand) will come together, their collective presence triggering the many layers of thought the practitioner brings to the working. A moment of quiet contemplation is appropriate at this point. Let your senses take in the colors, scents, and textures of your completed space. If you've added musical elements to the working, close your eyes and let those sounds help you relax and focus. When each breath comes and goes softly, almost without your awareness, you're ready to begin the specific spell you've entered this place to perform.

4. *Spellcasting:* By now, your spell is as familiar to you as any poem you ever memorized, any song that wormed its way into your head and left you humming snatches of it all day. Holding your desire at the forefront of your thoughts so you don't become too immured in the detail and forget the overall plan, work your way steadily through your chosen elements, whether spoken aloud or held silently in the heart. Don't stop. Find the rhythm of this working and let each part of it end naturally at the beginning of the next. Lighting a candle, for example, won't interfere with your spoken elements. When you're done, sit quietly and breathe easily. In the highly focused state brought on by ritual work, you are as receptive to inspiration as you will ever be. Wait and see if something connected to your efforts doesn't well quietly into your consciousness. If it does, store the images away for later consideration.

5. *Close the space:* As with preparing the space, there are two parts to closing it. One is the disassembling of the physical setup that preceded the working. Cleanse and store your tools. Make mental notes of the components you may have to replace. The second aspect is to dispel the protections you

raised before you began, and to release any lingering emotional and magical residue which might otherwise resurface in your next working. When you leave your space, you should feel calm and assured.

6. *Grounding:* Much of the preparation for spellcasting is designed to let the witch enter an altered state of consciousness where receptivity and intuition are emphasized. Much of the time *after* spellcasting is devoted to reconnecting with the physical world. Usually described as grounding, this period allows practitioners to eat if they've been fasting (actually good advice for all practitioners!), return to their everyday garb, and commit their response to the ritual to paper. The thoughts and ideas that surfaced after the spell was complete should be detailed now; you'll be surprised how easily they can slip away. Stray thoughts on how the working might be better done in future should be carefully entered in your *Book of Shadows.* The overall intention here is to integrate as much as possible of the spiritual experience with the witch's physical reality. Spending every moment in the heightened state of ritual awareness is simply impossible; actions taken during the grounding process allow the practitioner to continue learning even during periods of ordinary awareness.

With these steps as a framework, you have the beginning of just about any ritual you care to devise, although not all workings will require so elaborate a setup. Magical efforts can permeate any activity, and the opportunity to use less complex workings will arise more frequently as you learn to combine magical aims and simplify your rituals. Some spells require little more than the desire to accomplish a goal and the effort to clearly focus an intention. Many witches, for example, grow their own herbs and encourage healthy growth by simply visualizing what a strong plant will look like and holding that image while they touch, or weed around, their seedlings. Understanding the principles of ritual enable spontaneous workings; each step isn't exhibited in its fully realized form, but the skilled practitioner can still quickly visualize the entire process—a sort of magical shorthand that allows a single gesture to stand for all the ceremony normally included in, for example, warding a circle.

Among the very first spells taught to novice practitioners (and learned by wise solitary witches!) are spells of protection. Few real witches will find themselves under magical attack as regularly as the Halliwell sisters, but all prudent practitioners incorporate some version of a personal protection spell into their rituals. Not only does it afford a measure of safety (from everyday dangers as well as spiritual or magical perils), it also serves as a potent reminder that ritual work is not a game but a series of highly motivated actions which, like all actions, come with consequences. In addition to the preliminary steps in a longer ritual, protection spells may themselves be the focus of a working, as can the closely related spells of banishment or exorcism. While protection spells aim to prevent any malign beings (human or otherwise) from taking up residence, banishments and exorcisms take aim on unwanted influences that are already present or actively seeking to harm the practitioner. *Charmed* contains several examples of the later type.

In "Is There a Woogy in the House?," an evil entity has been hiding under the Halliwell house for decades, awaiting an opportunity to overtake at least one of its residents. Phoebe's magical response, learned from her grandmother, is a classic banishment.

> I am Light.
> I am one too strong to fight.
> Return to Dark, where Shadows dwell.
> You cannot have this Halliwell.
> Go away and leave my sight,
> And take with you this endless night.

Breaking this banishment down reveals a framework that underlies all ritual.

First, the self-awareness of the practitioner is established: "I am Light." In the shortest terms possible, the witch confirms that her motives are true and without selfish or evil intent.

"I am one too strong to fight" isn't a protective spell but certainly invokes the image of the practitioner inside some sturdy construct that won't permit this evil to enter, which is, after all, the end result of a spell of protection.

Without further preamble, this invocation continues with a direct statement of the witch's desire spelled out in terms that, like all good spellwork, can't be misconstrued. And, like all good rituals, this spell isn't an all-purpose recipe but a specific set of elements designed to have a specific effect on a specific target.

Keeping in mind the desirability of custom-fitting your spellwork to your desires, here are some other rites of protection and banishment that you can adapt to your own needs.

Protection from Gossip or Slander

As Prue discovers in "Murphy's Luck," not all attacks are outright physical assaults; some are much more insidious. In that episode, an undermining of her self-confidence left her alone and afraid, a perfect target. The threat to her good professional name was the immediate problem, and as the situation is as old as humanity itself, spells have evolved to protect against it.

For this rite, you should work within a protected space and prepare yourself by consciously working to dispel any anger or feelings of vengeance you may harbor against the individual speaking badly of you. The goal isn't to punish but to prevent. Inside your space, meditate quietly until you feel calm, then build a mental picture of the person you hope to affect. If you don't know exactly who the culprit is, build an image of the characteristics

When burying the hatchet doesn't seem to be working, try burying the spell cord instead.

that might be behind the gossip. Using a heavy cord in a color that speaks to either binding or protection, whichever appeals to your sensibilities, tie the ends while you imagine the gossip inside the circle (if a binding will fulfill your intention) or yourself inside the ring, if you chose to make yourself the focus of the ritual.

If you envision the rite as a binding, which works best if you know your opposition, turn the cord in your hands and create tiny loops in it as you identify the emotions that may be behind the harsh words. Envy? Picture yourself tying up the envy as you tie your loop. Bitterness? Prepare a loop for it. Continue until you've satisfied yourself that your opposite number is free of whatever influences might be urging him or her to such self-destructive actions. Now visualize the cord rising around this person, freeing him or her while retaining control of the influences that led to the slander or gossip. Keeping the free individual in front of your mind's eye, cast the cord onto a brazier, or ritually bury it in a cauldron of sand until you can burn it later.

If you can't summon up a clear image of the person, it might be easier to switch the focus to yourself, which you should be able to envision easily if you've been following a meditation schedule for even a short time. Now, instead of caging you in, the circle of cord should be visualized as an impenetrable barrier protecting you from the effects of gossip. As each hateful comment comes toward you, picture the cord curling up to capture it, and make your loops as before. Also catch any negative responses that you've felt emanate from you. Bind them all within the loops, then, once again, either burn the cord or bury it.

Some practitioners will save the ashes to scatter on the next breeze, dispelling their influence even more completely.

To Protect the Ritual Space: Casting the Triple Circle

Every witch wants to believe that he or she can practice in complete safety within their own space, if nowhere else. Many elaborate rituals have been created, several of which may appeal to your inner symbolism. The Triple Circle is believed to have been used as far back as the height of the Babylonian Empire, and both the clean simplicity of this working and its almost universal symbolism have ensured its survival in several magical traditions.

The first step is to delineate the space you wish to protect. Chalk, which comes from the earth, usually fulfills this part of the rite, during which a single circle large enough to enclose the practitioner and the work area is marked out. The importance of a continuous line, rather than a series of arcs, is to reinforce the symbolism of an unbroken wall. Not only do you want to keep harmful effects out, but you want to protect others outside your circle from accidently being affected by whatever rite you have prepared. For an example in Halliwellian-styled magic, you have only to think back to Prue's gender-changing spell in "She's a Man, Baby, a Man!" Crouched within her chalk circle, which also incorporates the universal symbol for masculinity, only she is affected—for which her sisters are, no doubt, grateful.

A simple cleansing ritual that can be done almost anywhere calls for salt to be spread around the area or person to be cleansed, while a candle set in the rest of the salt burns away.

Next, the space must be cleansed of any influences that might linger from previous workings or that are deliberately sent into the space by an outsider. For this casting, salt is the most traditional component. Salt helped preserve food, scoured eating and healing tools, and even cleansed the skin before the beneficial influence of soap, was established. If you think back to the self-exploration lesson on brooms, you may decide that the besom symbolism fits better into your vision of how to cleanse a work space.

Last, the athame, which represents the power you hope to bring to bear and the martial nature of the protection, is traced through the two previous circles. Don't lift your blade when you come to the join in your circle. Instead, picture the circles surrounding you as a line of light or strength; then, with the tip of your athame, "hook" the edge of the circle to pull it up and over your head, bringing the blade down to touch the circle again on the opposite side. A hemisphere of light may be an appropriate image for the result. Pause and stand straight, then hook the circle on the tip of the athame once more and sketch a line in the air that traces an identical hemisphere under your feet and back to the opposite side of the circle. In your mind's eye, you should be standing in the center of an orb of protective energy. To release the protection this spell affords, reverse the actions and imagery, remembering to break the physical circles as well as their equivalents on your mental landscape.

To Protect the Household

Some traditions of magical practice take the notion of a sacred space, whether called a covenstead, a homestead, or simply The House, a bit further than just the working circle by expanding the protection spells used to cover an entire home or property. This technique is most often used when a family tradition has seen generations of witches occupying the same property, or when a group of witches deliberately choose to live together and follow an active magical lifestyle, but the ritual is no less appropriate to the solitary practitioner who would like to ritually clean a new home or spring-clean their existing home.

You'll wish to have lots of candles on hand, and if your home is large, it wouldn't hurt to have a friend join you for the ritual working.

Find the center of your home, either its physical center or your working center, whichever feels right. Many practitioners start with the highest room in the house and work their way down (which would be doubly appropriate in, for example, the Halliwell house, as the highest room in the house also happens to be their work space), or start with the lowest rooms if they happen to be earthen-floored basements or cellars.

Light a blue candle anointed with the oil of bay leaves, or whichever plants have the strongest protective resonances for you, in that first room, and take a moment to form your intention while contemplating the flame and breathing the scent of the oils. Then, with a full-sized broom, proceed clockwise around the room while visualizing all negative emotions being

The essence of this spell is captured in a nursery school carol: "Bind a broom and burn one blue, bay's the leaf, see out, see you!"

pushed ahead of you. (Don't forget, your ritual broom isn't meant for sweeping floors! You're sweeping just above the floor, not on it.) Proceed in like fashion from room to room, always pushing the unwanted influences out of each room and down to the area just in front of the house's most often used exit. There, sweep three times across the threshold from inside to outside, then close the door. Hopefully, you'll complete this part of the ritual before any of your candles burn out!

After returning your broom to its ritual space, take up a full, fresh bay leaf (not a dried one out of the spice rack for this purpose) and walk the same route from room to room. At each candle, pass the leaf gently through the flame, then trace around any openings into the room: Windows and doors are obvious, but don't forget fireplace openings and any vents in the rooms as well. Back at the front door, trace the opening three times, then tuck the leaf away in a safe place until you repeat the spell in the future. At that time, you can ritually burn one leaf while taking up a new one.

Don't forget to let all your candles burn out in their own time.

A ritual with the same purpose, but more permanent in nature and covering an entire property, is the Rowan Walk. In areas where growing rowan trees is possible, the plantings described in this ritual are actual, not symbolic, and the entire ritual usually takes place in spring; but, as rowan won't grow everywhere, there's a version for urbanites and others who'd also like to enact this working at any time.

The rowan has long been held to offer protective shade to those who stand under it, and to that end, mothers often named a sickly child Rowan or Rowena in hopes of drawing on that safeguard. Rowan wood was also incorporated into the thresholds of doorways in older British Isle homes. Twigs of this wood, braided and tied with blue ribbons, have even been found tucked into wall spaces in older North American homes.

Begin by ascertaining the cardinal compass points on your property or within your apartment. Carefully inspect each outdoor site to ensure that any saplings planted there have a reasonable expectation of survival. Don't plant a sapling in the middle of your walkway, for example, just to satisfy this condition. If you don't have four suitable locations, simply move back inside and use the other version. If you do have four appropriate spots, gently turn enough soil to accommodate your trees, then drop something of yourself into each patch of prepared ground.

A single thread of hair will link you firmly to this earth and probably won't break down for the entire life of the tree. Leave the turned earth for several days while you soak the roots of your rowan saplings in water mixed with vervain leaves. Vervain, itself a plant with powerful protective associations, is believed to guard the rowan's roots from harmful insects or growths. This soaking should last for three days, the day of the full moon and the days immediately before and after.

As you plant the trees, wrap a single blue thread around each sapling's trunk. This thread will break as the plant grows, but symbolizes your intention to care for the rowan until it is established and it, in return, protects you and your home.

If you can't plant trees around your home, you can still shelter under their symbolic influence by collecting deadwood from a rowan and treating it in much the same way you would have treated the live plant. Instead of soaking just the roots in the vervain water, submerge the twigs completely. Three days later, they will be considerably more supple, ready for you to braid or twine together with blue thread or ribbons and, again, one of your hairs or other personal item. Make sure you have enough twigs to form four braids, then, after locating the cardinal compass points, hang the garlands in the four corners of your home.

Obviously, you can't live within the boundaries established by those four points forever, so, even if you've planted your trees instead of preparing rowan braids, you might like to make a tiny braid to carry in your pocket or your car.

Protection from a Specific Threat

Closely related to protection spells are spells to banish malevolent beings (human or otherwise). In "Thank You for Not Morphing," the Halliwell sisters discover that, despite the protections evidently bound up with their home, they've inadvertently allowed enemies inside. Their response is this brief incantation:

> When in the Circle that is Home,
> Safety's gone and evils roam,
> Rid all beings from these walls,
> We sisters three,
> Now heed our call.

In "The Power of Two," Jackson Ward is actively stalking his targets. Again, there is a vocal response, this time by Prue.

> Ashes to ashes, spirit to spirit,
> Take his soul, banish this evil!

While an outright exorcism is often accompanied by considerable ritual, including a variety of protection and containment spells, banishment is generally an immediate response to a particular situation and involves little preparation. Most likely to be a spontaneous working, the outward rites may be nothing more

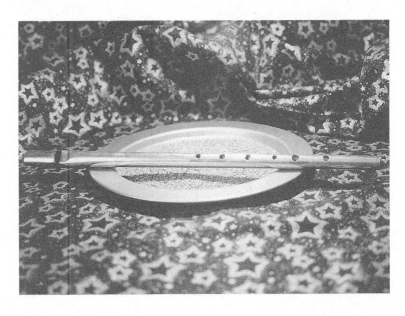

Poppies held an unusual place in exorcism rites in what is now Thailand. Smoking poppy was believed to induce hallucinations and disturb the ghosts of any nearby bodies. The only way to lay those shades to rest was to burn poppy seeds over their graves.

than a quick invocation that includes a clear statement of the witch's desire, but even this abbreviated version assumes that the spellcaster performed some sort of shorthand protection spell along the way, if only a quick visualization of him- or herself inside the protected space.

A number of banishments have been collected over the years, from those addressed to the vague sense of presence or depression that can permeate a home to invocations that presume the presence of an evil being. This gentler version takes for granted that any emotional residue left behind is unintentional, not an outright attack on any specific person.

To Banish the Remnants of Another Personality

Your time is passed.
We know you not.
Here you are lost.
Go from us now.
Find your new place.
There, look upon a loved one's face.

Rewind the threads of a life now passed.
Waste no glance back, countenance no lapse.

Cast light upon this wandering shadow,
Meet no more, now or tomorrow.

Your time is passed.

While the invocation is clearly stated (if not well rhymed or metered, after translation from the French) and should be sufficient expression of your desire, additional symbolism can reinforce the purpose of the working. Lighting and carrying a black candle through the affected area is symbolic of change. Burning poppy seed is believed to satiate emotional remnants and send them to a more permanent rest. The chiming of bells or playing of metal instruments has the opposite effect, waking the scattered bits of personality to their situation and sending them away, carried on the bell's peals to a more appropriate place.

The stronger forms of exorcism and banishment, by their very existence, support the belief that evil demons, spirits, or individuals exist and have power. Not all witches embrace such beliefs; most don't, which explains the relatively few modern spells addressing disincarnate, wandering spirits. The *Charmed* episodes "I've Got You Under My Skin" and "The Witch Is Back," despite being fictional, probably provide as effective a pair of invocations as any.

> Evil eyes, look unto thee
> May they soon extinguished be.
> Bend they will to the power of three,
> Eye of earth, evil and accursed.
> > —*The Halliwell sisters,*
> > *"I've Got You Under My Skin"*

> Outside of time,
> Outside of gain.
> Know only sorrow,
> Know only pain.
> > —*Melinda Warren,*
> > *"The Witch Is Back"*

Spells of Love

Just as life revolves around love and relationships of all kinds, so too do many magical rituals focus on getting, increasing, or keeping various kinds of love. Unlike banishment spells, which are usually cast on the spot with little or no accompanying ritual, spells about love are highly ritualized. Why? Because even if we all assume that love is a good thing, the witch who seeks to change another's feelings must be very sure of her motives, or her spells can easily edge over into selfishness or even outright coercion. Ritual provides ample opportunity for sober second thoughts.

To alleviate some of those concerns, most so-called love spells aren't directed at any particular individual. For a Halliwellian example, remember the ritual Piper and Phoebe enact in "Dream Sorcerer." Upstairs in their usual work space, the girls prepare by collecting the cauldron, herbs, and candles, preliminary steps that provide lots of time for contemplation. The main component of their ritual, a written list of the qualities they hope to bring into their lives, also requires considerable thought. The simplicity of the vocal element, when compared to the other, highly stylized, parts of the ritual, indicates that most of the important visualization actually occurs *before* the spell is cast. In fact, as a statement of will and desire, this particular love spell is about as brief as it gets.

These spells are no more than road maps for a considerate spellcaster. Changing an element to one more evocative for yourself is all part of the process. You can't really do it wrong.

> I conjure Thee.
> I conjure Thee.
> I'm the Queen.
> You're the Bee.
> As I desire, so shall it be!

Contrary to the generality of that spell is the very specific wording used in "Something Wicca This Way Comes" to *rid* Piper of a distinctly unwanted lover.

Your love wither and depart,
from my life and from my heart.
Let me be, Jeremy,
And go away, forever.

In both instances, however, substantial preparation accompanies the ritual. In an attempt to pry Jeremy out of Piper's life, a fairly ornate poppet, a human-shaped doll, is created, and the red roses that often symbolize love are procured to help focus intentions.

"Animal Pragmatism" provides yet another example of how love spells, even those intended to be temporary, or undertaken within a ritual setting, or only general in scope, can go utterly wrong. However, some witches would reasonably argue that anyone trying to turn snakes and bunnies into full, equal partners was going about things all wrong, anyway! The spells collected here are all aimed at less transitory types of love, but these too should, like all spells, be adapted to your own symbolism and intentions. Remember, the more thought you put into a working before it is attempted, the more likely it is to accomplish what you really desire.

To Become Lovable

Knowing what you want in a partner is an important part of finding the right one. If you know your own standards and stick to them, you can't be lured into relationships that are detrimental and prevent you from enjoying a positive relationship with someone else. The other half of finding the "perfect" partner is *being* the person that individual would be attracted to. This spell encourages self-examination to help you overcome any feelings that you are somehow not worthy of that partner, to help you stick to your standard and not "settle," thereby losing the opportunity to meet Mr. or Ms. Right.

Inside your warded circle, where you are most safe and can open your heart without fear, prop your mirror on your altar and light an appropriately colored candle. Allow the light from the candle to illuminate your face as you look into your mirror. Breathe lightly on the mirror to momentarily fog its surface and, as your image becomes visible once again, recognize this opportunity to see yourself as a new person in your life would see you. Ignore the color of your eyes or the shape of your nose in favor of your expression. Are there more laugh lines or frown lines? Is the smile you direct at yourself wide and joyful or hesitant and a bit shy? How easily do you meet your own eyes in the mirror?

Looking past that image—close your eyes if you need to—build a mental picture of all the qualities that might stand in the way of finding your love. Does fear prevent you from offering a smile when you meet someone new? Does a lack of confidence impede your efforts to meet people? Are old hurts dragging you down? Now, take all these negative aspects and picture them dwindling down to a spot no bigger than the nail on your little finger, then tuck it away in your heart. Why not visualize yourself losing those traits altogether? Because compassion and empathy arise from shared experience. Throwing away that experience denies a part of yourself and may, ultimately, make you *less* able to relate to others.

Opening your eyes again, draw your candle close enough to reflect in the mirror, then let these words form your intention.

> Let all inner doubts go free,
> Let the lover come to me,
> I'll let my true self for him (or her) unfold,
> Let myself know joy untold.

With that, return to your meditations as your candle burns away.

The purpose of this spell, like most well-intentioned magical workings, is not to force change on another, but to encourage self-realization that is perceptible to others. Confident people are attracted to other confident people. Compassionate people seldom are happy with anyone less likely to reach out to others. Opposites may pull magnets together, but you give yourself a better chance at love by being the type of person others like to love.

To Bring Like-minded People into Your Life

Just as lovable people tend to be loved, you're most likely to find a life partner among people who share your interests. The common cry among those seeking a new relationship is "All the best people are already taken!" This next rite is intended to do no more than attract those who share your beliefs, interests, and enthusiasms. As is often the case with love spells, this one works indirectly. It's still up to you to find, among those people so drawn, the one who could partner you for life. In one sense, it's a win-win situation. Even if you don't find the perfect mate right away, you're likely to make a lot of new friends!

First fill a bowl with fresh water and carry it into a naturally lit location where you can sit comfortably and watch the surface until you are centered, ready to invite other people into your life. Envision the activities you'd like to share, the things that *you* plan to bring to the relationship. When you're completely focused, take up a handful of dried rose hips and let them fall randomly onto the water. Roses are symbolic of adult love; the seeds within the hips represent the first stirring of that love. Wrapping your hands around the bowl, watch the hips bob slowly across the surface. In time, if there are like-minded people nearby who might become known to you, the hips will gradually float together, much as droplets of oil eventually form a single mass. Let your vision focus a little beyond the water's surface at that point, and softly repeat this phrasing, or one suitable to your true desire.

As within, so without.
I put aside all lingering doubt.
The call I send is pure,
It comes with love to reassure.
If towards me you would draw,
I'd allow my heart brief thaw.
If in partnership we meet,
Then love will in our hearts be mete.

If you are in the wrong place, if there is simply no one in your area who could fulfill your desire, the hips will continue to bob about independently.

To Find Love

Have you heard the phrase "There's someone for everyone"? If you've been frustrated in love, you've probably added a mental caveat along the lines of "Yes, in Timbuktu!"

Many people believe that each life supports just one true love, and if that person never happens to be in our vicinity, we'll go through life either settling for a relationship that doesn't feel quite right, or simply alone. This next love spell isn't to be undertaken lightly, but for the person who feels he or she must go to the mountain (the mountain having shown no signs of moving to them), it does give some direction to the search.

First, cast the circle to ensure that no undue influences disturb this ritual. Divinations, by their nature, rely on the vaguest of clues to provide a correct answer, so don't leave yourself open to uncontrolled suggestions by operating outside a circle. Next, dress your altar in colors that seem appropriate to you. The reds of love and the paler pinks of friendship may appear good choices; so too might the black and white of opposites attracting. Cover the entire altar with a map of the territory to which you'd be willing to travel if you could find love. For some, this may suggest the use of a world map, while for others, a narrower focus may be more realistic.

Anchor the corners of the map with red tapers and surround yourself with scents designed to reflect the love you seek and open your heart and mind to intuition. Acacia might fulfill both requirements. Prepare a pendulum from a crystal associated with love or divining, or from an object that represents love to you. Holding your desire at the forefront of your thoughts, allow the pendulum to swing easily from the tips of your fingers over the entire area. A slight tugging will indicate the correspondence of your desire and the place where that desire may be fulfilled.

Keeping your thoughts open and your breathing even, fold the map in half and repeat the process, allowing the pendulum to narrow your field again. Continue to fold the map until the pendulum no longer indicates a preference for any section, and that is where you will find love. As the candles burn away, meditate on what a move to that location might mean, and honestly assess your commitment to following the pendulum's suggestion.

THE WORKING ELEMENT

A Personal Growth Exercise

Some of the banishments undertaken by the Halliwells have been examples of spontaneous ritual, a sort of guerrilla spellcasting that might leave the impression that defensive spells are ritual-less. Yet, when a specific individual was to be banished in "The Witch Is Back," considerable ritual was undertaken — as much as was required for a love spell! How might a witch's familiarity with her subject affect her ritual? Would knowing a specific person as the target of a spell seem to require more or less contemplation before taking action?

Protection, banishment, and love rites probably comprise fully half of all spells ever composed, but spells for wealth, health, and even luck at job interviews do exist. You'll likely find even wider applications for your growing knowledge of ritual, but for now, here are a broad spectrum of spells to serve as a jumping-off point for your own work.

To Empower Yourself for a Job Interview

Phoebe Halliwell's answer to the stresses of skill-testing questions at a job interview in "Painted World" is to create her first original spell ritual, of which this delightful—if badly scanned—invocation was part:

> Spirits, send the words,
> From all across the land.
> Allow me to absorb them,
> Through the touch of either hand.
> For twenty-four hours,
> From seven to seven,
> I will understand all meaning,
> Of the words from here to heaven.

For those of us whose usual problem during interviews is a virulent case of the stuttering heebie-jeebies, this ritual is designed to enhance communication.

Find a stone or crystal small enough to fit in a pocket or conceal in one hand and bring it into your ritual space. Set the stone in the middle of your altar as you choose two candles in whichever colors speak to you of communication and authority, traditionally blue and deepest purple. You might like to add a third candle in the yellow of success. Anoint your candles with one of the astringent oils symbolic of fresh beginnings. Lemon verbena, cinnamon, or any mint will clear your mind. As the scents float around you, consider what you can bring to the position and what you may learn from this experience as you breathe the oils.

When you feel calm, light your candles and pass your stone briefly through each flame as you envision it being charged with these characteristics, then hold the stone in your hands as the candles burn away.

Leave your stone on your altar until the day of your interview, then tuck it in your pocket or conceal it in one hand (not the one you'd normally shake hands with!). Visualize this stone or crystal as a miniature version of your work space. In its presence, you are safe and confident of your abilities. Touch the stone once at the beginning of the interview and again whenever you feel nervous. Picture the quiet authority you've vested in this object flowing out to surround you, then be yourself.

To Bless a Business Venture

If you've decided you're ready to employ yourself—it's not a choice for everyone, but at least you needn't be nervous during the interview!—this spell will draw success to your venture.

Start this ritual inside a properly warded work space. As *Charmed* reiterates on an almost weekly basis, rites designed for personal gain are temptations that should be examined carefully before beginning. As you cast the circle, consider the impact your business will have on your community and yourself. Will your business be a positive influence in your neighborhood? What can you incorporate into your business to ensure that something is given back, regularly, to the people who support it? Is this venture meant to make you a more well-rounded person, or just a wealthier person?

Inside the circle, light an open-style brazier and scatter a coarse mixture of bay, orange, and pomegranate leaves over the coals as you softly recite, "Luck, work, and passion." You must be

Yes, there really is a penny under there!

willing to bring these things to your new venture. Now, light a white candle from the embers of the brazier and set it atop a penny centered on your altar. As the wax coats the coin, let it remind you that while a living wage is important, so too are the ethics and motives that will come into play as you conduct the business of making a living.

When the candle has burned away, keep the penny until your business opens, then leave it on the premises to continue its quiet job.

To Ask for Guidance

Sometimes magic isn't an end but rather the means to an end. When you don't want a full-fledged miracle and are just looking for a hint, a bit of otherworldly advice, you're entering the realm of lesser divinations. If the dedicated divinatory arts like the Tarot, the I Ching, or the Runes seem a little much for a simple "Should I or shouldn't I?" in front of the cookie jar at midnight, a sign is as good as a high-definition, surround-sound vision.

a time for spells

Phoebe realizes this when she devises a spell in her bathroom in the opening scenes of "Give Me a Sign."

> I beseech all powers above,
> Send a sign to free my sister's heart,
> One that will lead her to her love.

The rest of the episode goes on to emphasize how unreliable signs (or maybe just spells cast in bathrooms) are!

Just because signs aren't as spectacular as curses, telekinesis, or stopping time in its tracks doesn't mean that the same preparation isn't a prerequisite. What's the point in asking for a sign without having any idea how the request might be answered? Experience and practice count as much in this kitchen magic as in ritual divination, but until you've gained enough knowledge to discriminate between the overheard comment that *might* contain the answer to your question and one half of a phone conversation about bunions, you'll find these next four rites priceless. Unlike Phoebe's spell, they all limit the source of signs to a single medium. They're all simple yes/no diviners, however, so recognize that limitation when you begin.

SIGNED IN AIR

If your contemplations lead you to walk where birds shed feathers, anywhere from a beach to a crowded city park, take the opportunity to gather one dark and one light feather on your next stroll. Some practitioners swear by one raven's feather plus one from any bird in its winter plumage, but any two feathers that can be easily separated from each other should suffice. The lighter feather will symbolize a "yes" response while the darker or black feather is a "no."

Place both feathers on your altar, one to each side. Lay your athame between them and spin it firmly as you ask your question. If the blade points to the black feather, the answer is no; if to the white feather, the answer is yes. If the blade doesn't point at either feather, there is no answer possible just now.

SIGNED IN WATER

Set an ordinary wineglass with a capacity larger than your chalice outside during the night of a full moon. Do not touch the glass again until it is completely filled with rainwater. While you wait for nature to determine when you'll finish this rite, locate an elder tree and gather a leaf already fallen to the ground. When the rain has filled your glass, bring it inside your work space and fill your chalice completely; a small amount of water should be left in the bottom of the wineglass. Light a small blue taper.

Place yourself directly in front of your altar and gently lay your leaf in the center of the water in the chalice. The leaf should be small enough to float freely without touching the rim. Drink the last of the water as you recall your question, then lay your hands on the foot of the chalice and allow yourself to fall into light meditation on the question. When the candle has burned away, examine the leaf. If it is now touching the rim of the chalice, your answer is yes; if not, the answer is no. If the leaf sinks before the candle has guttered out naturally, no answer is possible at this time.

SIGNED IN EARTH

Perhaps the simplest of the elemental sign rites is the drawing of stones. Find seven dark stones and seven light, all of the same basic size and shape. This task may take you some time, but most practitioners find several uses for the stones. Fill your cauldron with sand and bury the stones beneath the surface one by one, asking your question as each stone disappears. Then light a small white taper and meditate before your altar as you wait for it to burn away. Smooth the surface of the sand and, with your eyes closed, turn the cauldron clockwise three times. Keeping the question in mind, let your fingers work through the sand and

For really detailed replies to an earth request, you might consider using a set of rune stones instead of these very simple magics.

draw the third stone your fingers encounter. If the stone is dark, the answer is no; if light, yes.

A variant of this rite allows a more gradated response than yes or no. Instead of finding seven dark and seven light, the diviner looks for seven stones of various degrees of dark and light. One stone will be a middle tone, the neutral response; three lighter stones will be varying degrees of yes; and the three darker stones will be everything from "Probably not a plan" to "Not on your life!"

SIGNED IN FIRE

While fire has figured to some degree in the other divinations, mostly as a keeper of time, it is the sole source of inspiration in

Incense and oils, one of the more pleasant ways of adding the element of fire to a ritual.

this ritual. Your altar should be bare of everything except three candles: one white, one black, and one gray. All the tapers should be of equal size, but not so large that you'll be meditating for hours as they burn out. (Perhaps Phoebe is on to something when she substitutes a birthday candle for the more traditional pillar in "Something Wicca This Way Comes.")

Cast your circle as usual. Inside the circle, anoint each of your candles with rosemary oil and an oil that seems appropriate to your question. Light the candles and use each flame as a focus point for your meditations. As you consider the white candle, try to picture the positive actions that might flow from the

Charmed's auction house, appropriately, is called Buckland's. Raymond Buckland has dozens of books on magic and the occult, among them: *Buckland's Complete Book of Witchcraft, Ray Buckland's Magick Cauldron,* and *Buckland's Gypsy Fortune-telling Deck.* Researching a show on witches would be difficult, if not impossible, *without* seeing Ray Buckland's name!

answer you're seeking. Acknowledge the negative aspects of your choices while looking through the flame of the black candle; while contemplating the gray candle, which should hold the center position on your altar, ask if this is the time to make such a choice and what might be the result of making no decision at all just yet.

The last candle to burn itself out is your answer.

Finding the Right Day

Because much magical ritual is based in sympathetic workings—the belief that affecting one thing also affects those with the same characteristics—timing for many spells turns on the phase of the moon or day of the week or season, which is, at least in part, a reflection of the influence astrology has held over magical ritual. Luckily, you don't need to know everything there is to know about astrology before beginning to add some of its layered meanings to your own rituals.

DAY	COLORS	CORRESPONDENCES
Friday	Blue	Relationships between adults: friendship, love, and passion
Saturday	Black/Dark Blue	Banishment, protection, inner strength
Sunday	Yellow	Familial relationships
Monday	White	Inspiration, creativity, intuition, dreams, divination
Tuesday	Red	Problems, conflicts, resolutions
Wednesday	Purple	Duality, communication, partnerships
Thursday	Green	Money, wealth, prosperity, work, healing

The Elemental Correspondences

To decide which of the requests for a sign might be best suited to your question, it's helpful to know what each element has stood for traditionally.

WATER: Relates to the emotions, psychic phenomenon, intuition, and the color blue. It is most often symbolized by bowls and chalices, mirrors, and seashells. Astrologically, the signs Cancer, Pisces, and Scorpio also represent water. So, too, do the Tarot suit Cups and the direction west.

EARTH: Relates to material things like money, business, work, but also fertility and abundance. Symbolism is, not surprisingly, associated with earthy things like crystals, sand, stones, coins, metals, and herbs. Deepest green, brown, and black are associated with the element earth. The signs Capricorn, Virgo, and Taurus are all earth signs. In a Tarot deck, the Pentacles, which often speak to matters involving money, are linked to earth, as is the direction north.

AIR: This most ephemeral of the elements relates to communication, thought, travel, and the intellectual pursuits. Its symbolism is drawn from those things that alert us to air's presence, even if we can see only the result of its presence and not air itself: feathers, smoke and incense, chimes, bells, and empty bowls. Because air is often associated with the sun, its color is generally yellow, but gray, the color of smoke, is another frequent choice. Astrologically, Gemini, Aquarius, and Libra are connected to air. If you choose a Tarot suit to represent this element, Swords would be an appropriate choice and can be represented on your altar by the athame. Air is usually associated with the east.

FIRE: Fire's many associations include sexual love and energy, inspiration, change, transmutation, reincarnation; in its role as the focus of the hearth, it corresponds to home and family. Its symbolism includes incense, fire, burning candles, and red is the color associated with this element. Aries, Leo, and Sagittarius are all fire signs. Wands, both the ritual tools and the Tarot suit, can represent fire in your workings. Facing the south is yet another way of invoking this element.

The
Observant
Witch

ecause the first lesson of all esoteric paths is learning to see, to grasp what is hidden or invisible, to notice what others miss, this section is a guide to a new level of multilevel awareness. Taking each *Charmed* episode in order, we'll make note of its magical significance, which traditions are being explored, and which legends re-created. Having read the preceding chapters, you'll be able to view these episodes with new eyes and decide what lessons, magical or otherwise, you can adapt to your own practice. But don't stop there. After you've watched once, and think you've taken everything you can from that viewing, turn to the end of the section and see how many of the bloopers listed there you caught. Perhaps you'll be able to add some of your own!

Season One

REMEMBER WHEN . . .

. . . On her first night back in the family home, Phoebe Halliwell discovers a *Book of Shadows* in the attic and, chanting the first incantation, revives the power of the Charmed Ones in herself and her unwitting sisters?

MAGICAL NOTES

This episode establishes most of the rules for the *Charmed* version of witchcraft, everything from the Wiccan Rede of the real world to the mythos of the Charmed Ones' televised universe.

It's also the first time we see the spirit board in use. Although Grams Halliwell is later established as the one flicking the pages of the *Book of Shadows*, no explanation was ever given for the movement of the spirit board pointer. Grams, too? An early, different manifestation of Phoebe's power? Or something else?

Original airdate: October 14, 1998

Guests:

Julie Araskas (Darlene)

Leigh-Allyn Baker (Hannah Webster)

Ben Caswell (Max Jones)

Todd Feder (Clerk)

Lou Glenn (Carpenter)

Cynthia King

Tamara Lee Krinsky (Tia)

Bailey Lueigert

Ralph Manza (Elderly man)

Michael Philip (Stefan)

Barbara Pilavin

Neil Roberts (Rex Buckland)

Marc Shelton

REMEMBER WHEN . . .

. . . Young women, innocents, were being abducted all over San Francisco, bringing Andy Trudeau and Darryl Morris into the search for a photographer who has taken a more than skin-deep interest in Phoebe. Meanwhile, Prue is distracted by the search for a new job and by her night with Andy; Piper, by a rising fear that her powers come from some evil source.

MAGICAL NOTES

An increasing percentage of those who define themselves as witches are calling their craft a lifestyle, not a religion. They claim it is a path to greater awareness—like yoga, or transcendental meditation—not through the agency of some outside power but through their own knowledge, study, and will. How does *Charmed*'s balance of the religion/lifestyle issue fit with your thoughts?

TITLE   **"THANK YOU FOR NOT MORPHING" 1-03**

Writers: Chris Levinson and Zach Estrin
Director: Ellen Pressman
Original airdate: October 21, 1998
Guests: Tony Denison (Victor Halliwell)
                  James Dineen (Mailman)
                  Markus Flanagan (Marshall)
                  Brian Krause (Leo Wyatt)
                  Eric Matheny (Fritz)
                  Mariah O'Brien (Cynda)

REMEMBER WHEN . . .

. . .Victor Halliwell, the sisters' father, returned after a twenty-year absence? Greeted with both anticipation and suspicion by his daughters, he remains all too curious about their developing powers and the *Book of Shadows*, leaving them divided and vulnerable when they most need unity to ward off attacks from an unexpected source.

MAGICAL NOTES

In describing her father's ring, Prue speaks of duality, the balance of male and female. While Wiccan philosophy tends to concentrate on trinity principles, such as the concept of Maiden, Mother, and Crone—as well as on triplet philosophies, such as the Threefold Law, which states that what a Wiccan does comes back three-fold—more traditional witchcraft emphasizes duality, opposition, and balance: light and dark, male and female, the god and the goddess. How does Piper's assertion that powers (the Charmed Ones' special powers, at least) are a "chick thing" fit into these ideologies?

TITLE	"DEAD MAN DATING" 1-04
Writer:	Javier Grillo-Marxuach
Director:	Richard Compton
Original airdate:	October 28, 1998
Guests:	John Cho (Mark Chao)
	Randelle Grenachia (Frankie)
	Patricia Harty (Mrs. Correy)
	Joe Hoe (Tony Wong)
	William Francis McGuire (Nick Correy)
	Todd Newton
	Sherrie Rose (Susan Trudeau)
	Elizabeth Sung (Mrs. Chao)

REMEMBER WHEN . . .

. . . Mark Chao was murdered to provide a corpse that his killers hoped would convince police that local gangster Tony Wong had died instead? Only the witches could see Mark's restless ghost or put this wrong right before Yahma, a Chinese demigod, arrived to carry off the disembodied soul.

MAGICAL NOTES

From the first episode, much has been made of the consequences of casting spells for personal gain: it's a karmic no-no. The same, however, doesn't seem to be true for their powers—sliding a dessert cart into an ex-boyfriend's path isn't exactly an example of altruistic behavior. How would you define "personal gain"?

TITLE	"DREAM SORCERER" 1-05
Writer:	Constance M. Burge
Director:	Nick Marck
Original airdate:	November 4, 1998
Guests:	Bo Clancy (Businessman)
	Rainoldo Gooding (Guy #1)
	Tim Herzog (Hans)

James Howell (Technician #1)

Todd Howk (E.R. nurse)

Alex Mendoza (Jack Manford)

J. Robin Miller (Skye Russell)

Marie O'Donnell (Dr. Black)

James O'Shea (Goatee guy)

Neil Roberts (Rex Buckland)

Matt Schulze (Whitaker Berman)

Doug Spearman (Nurse)

Trish Suhr (Paramedic #1)

REMEMBER WHEN...

...Thanks to a dream researcher's nocturnal mental wanderings, women who die in their dreams are dying for real. The investigation of those deaths got complex when Andy was assigned the case and Prue became the killer's next target.

MAGICAL NOTES

Dreams continue to defy explanation by current science. We know we have them, but we have no idea how or why. Esoteric practice has always believed dreams to be gateways to other forms of consciousness, other realms of thought. Particularly vibrant or persistent dreams are often thought to be prophetic. Commit your most vivid dream to paper, recalling as many details as possible. Come back to visit that description in a month, then in a year. Are your dreams prophetic? Or merely random bursts of mental static?

TITLE "THE WEDDING FROM HELL" 1-06

Writers:	Greg Elliot and Michael Perricone
Director:	R. W. Ginty
Original airdate:	November 11, 1998
Guests:	Roy Abramsohn (Doctor)
	Jennifer S. Badger (Bridesmaid #1)
	Leigh-Allyn Baker (Hannah Webster)

Todd Cattell (Elliot Spencer)

Deeny Consiglio (Kirsten)

Thomas Crawford (Security Guard #2)

Bill Ferrell (Security Guard)

Leon Franco (Male Stripper)

James Geralden (Justice of the peace)

Jeffrey Hutchinson (Father Trask)

David Moreland (Butler/Charles)

Phoenix Nugent (Seamstress)

Sara Rose Peterson (Jade D'Mon/Hecate)

Neil Roberts (Rex Buckland)

Christie Lynn Smith (Allison Michaels)

Barbara Stock (Mrs. Grace Spencer)

Eileen Weisinger (Bridesmaid #2)

REMEMBER WHEN . . .

. . . An inadvertent catering booking left Piper and her sisters on the spot when a priest is killed amid preparations for the society wedding of the year? Canapes came second to uncovering the demonic bride who'd pushed aside the groom's true love in her quest to marry a human lover and breed the ultimate demon child.

MAGICAL NOTES

Hecate, a goddess of the waning moon, is often interpreted as a witch goddess. In Asia Minor, she was an earth goddess, though she is best known for her role in the Greek tale of Demeter and Persephone, her daughter. Hades, god of the underworld, saw Persephone picking flowers, became enamored of her and kidnapped her, dragging her away to his underground kingdom. Only through the agency of Hecate, who lured the girl back to the surface before Persephone could eat enough food to bind her to the underworld forever, was Persephone able to negotiate a deal that allowed her to return to her mother for part of each year. (Demeter's misery at Persephone's annual descent into the underworld at that time is reflected in the season of winter; her joy at Persephone's return in the season of summer.) Hardly the horrible figure of Jade D'Mon.

TITLE	"THE FOURTH SISTER" 1-07
Writer:	Edithe Swenson
Director:	Gil Adler
Original airdate:	November 18, 1998
Guests:	Rebecca Balding (Aunt Jackie)
	Rebekah Carlton (Kali)
	Danielle Harris (Aviva)
	Brian Krause (Leo Wyatt)
	Michael LeBlanc (Video clerk)

REMEMBER WHEN...

...The sisters' amorous pursuits were interrupted by the reappearance of the cat, Kit, in the arms of Aviva, a troubled young woman with witchy powers of her own? Before long, the Halliwells were fighting among themselves over how much they could entrust to their newfound "colleague," a question that quickly became academic when Aviva started tossing fireballs at them!

MAGICAL NOTES

Mirrors, as gateways, are traditional tools in the practice of magic. Seen as windows to other worlds, a means of communicating both thoughts and words, useful for the storage of incidental power raised during other rituals, and for divination, mirrors are often kept close to work spaces. In this episode, the mirror is the channel through which Aviva and Kali communicate. How might a mirror be adapted for spell work aimed at contacting an inner self?

"THE TRUTH IS OUT THERE...
AND IT HURTS" 1-08

Writers:	Zack Estrin and Chris Levinson
Director:	Jim Contner
Original airdate:	November 25, 1998
Guests:	Leigh-Allyn Baker (Hannah Webster)
	Michelle Brookhurst (Tanya Parker)
	Richard Gilbert-Hill (Martin)
	Brad Greenquist (Gavin)
	Brian Krause (Leo Wyatt)
	Neil Roberts (Rex Buckland)
	Jason Stuart (Dr. Oliver Mitchell)
	Craig Thomas (Alex Pearson)

REMEMBER WHEN...

...Phoebe's precognitive power, working overtime, revealed the danger Gavin, a warlock from the future, held for a young woman in this time. Before she can take decisive action, both she and Piper are caught in the backwash of a truth spell—and how he'd respond to learning she's a witch.

MAGICAL NOTES

A number of forms of divination can be adapted for use as "truth spells." Asking whether something is true is as valid a question as any other. What credence should you lend to such answers, though? What factors might affect the answer? Would it be possible to narrow your questions and eliminate some of those variables? Might this be one case where the ability to know doesn't equate with a *right* or *need* to know? Nostradamus wrote, "All I thought I knew is nought, and truth no sop, when the roads of possibilities, opened, are left to me." Does Prue's use of this spell perhaps result in what Nostradamus feared, a self-fulfilling prophecy?

TITLE   "THE WITCH IS BACK" 1-09

Writer: Sheryl J. Anderson
Director: Richard Denault
Original airdate: December 16, 1998
Guests: Leigh-Allyn Baker (Hannah Webster)
                   Terry Bozeman (Arnold Halliwell)
                   Jodi Fung (TV reporter)
                   Brian Krause (Leo Wyatt)
                   Catherine Kwong (Waitress)
                   Tyler Layton (Melinda Warren)
                   Michael Mitz (Café patron)
                   Neil Roberts (Rex Buckland)
                   Billy Wirth (Matthew Tate)

REMEMBER WHEN...

...Three hundred years after Halliwell ancestress Melinda Warren trapped a warlock in a locket, Prue's touch freed Matthew Tate once more, to finish stealing all the Charmed Ones' powers. Deciding to go with experience over experimentation in ridding themselves of this menace, the sisters cast a spell to bring Melinda Warren into their time to repeat her original spell.

MAGICAL NOTES

In this episode, Phoebe discovers two important things about their magical journey: first, that they have the ability to create new spells for themselves; and second, that even good witches have cast curses in the *Charmed* universe.

The traditional followers of witchcraft have no Wiccan Rede or Threefold Law to determine whether or not their actions, physical or magical, are ethical. No spell is "good" or "bad"; that determination is made solely on the intent of the witch. How might this apply to Melinda Warren's curse? Might such a philosophy permit too much latitude for a spell worker? How might such apparent freedom be reasonably constrained?

TITLE   "WICCA ENVY" 1-10

Writers: Brad Kern and Sheryl J. Anderson

Director: Mel Damski

Original airdate: January 13, 1998

Guests: Leigh-Allyn Baker (Hannah Webster)

              Brian Krause (Leo Wyatt)

              Neil Roberts (Rex Buckland)

              Al Rodrigo (Security Guard Hymie)

              Tim Stark (Super)

REMEMBER WHEN . . .

. . . Confounded by their numerous previous schemes to steal the Halliwell powers, Rex Buckland and partner, Hannah Webster, Prue's bosses at Buckland's Auction House, take a more direct route, employing decidedly more mortal tools—like Andy Trudeau—and more prosaic means—like planting a stolen tiara in Prue's possession.

MAGICAL NOTES

As this episode so clearly illustrates, witches, like everyone else, must live in the real world as well as the arcane. Blending the two isn't always easy. Just as gays and lesbians frequently have difficulty identifying themselves as such in public, even to family and friends, witches often choose to hide their lifestyle from others. It's resulted in a play on words, "coming out of the broom closet," to describe the choice to live openly as a witch. If you were to begin incorporating elements of magic and ritual into your life, would you be a broom-closet witch or an "outed" witch? What would influence your choice?

TITLE   "FEATS OF CLAY" 1-11

Writers: Michael Perricone, Greg Elliot, Chris Levinson, and Zack Estrin

Story by: Javier Grillo-Marxuach

Director:	Kevin Inch
Original airdate:	January 20, 1999
Guests:	Eddie Bowz (Wesley)
	Victor Browne (Clay)
	Allen Cutler (Doug)
	Stacy Haiduk (The Guardian of the Urn)
	Allan Hunt (Auctioneer)
	Niklaus Lange (Palmer Kellogg)
	Ming Lo (Police officer)
	Carolyne Lowery (Sheila)(Shelley)
	Sean Moran (Customs officer)
	Cristine Rose (Claire Price)

REMEMBER WHEN . . .

. . . Clay, one of Phoebe's former lovers, arrived in San Francisco with a valuable urn for Prue to evaluate and auction. Phoebe's visions led her to hope he was there to renew their old romance, but the death of two of Clay's "associates" under unusual circumstances bodes poorly for all three sisters.

MAGICAL NOTES

This episode brings home time and again that, in some cases, events just have to run their own course and that magic isn't the answer to everything. What sort of deliberation might help identify those times for you?

TITLE   "THE WENDIGO" 1-12

Writer:	Edithe Swenson
Director:	James L. Conway
Original airdate:	February 3, 1999
Guests:	Charles Chun (Laurence Beck)
	William Dixon (E.R. doctor)
	Billy Jayne (Billy Waters)
	Christina Milian (Teri Lane)

Cristine Rose (Claire Price)

Jocelyn Seagrave (Agent Ashley Fallon)

J. Karen Thomas (Harriet Lane)

Richard S. Wolf (Auctioneer)

REMEMBER WHEN . . .

. . . After being attacked in a city park by an entity called a wendigo, Piper found herself taking on its animalistic attributes. An entry in the *Book of Shadows* explains that the only way to cure Piper was to track down and kill the creature that scratched her.

MAGICAL NOTES

It was once thought that witches could take on the aspect of various animals at will, a belief that's commonly held of the Native American shamans known as skin walkers, the Zimbabwean akiea, and many others. For what purpose might a witch of any type want this ability?

TITLE	"FROM FEAR TO ETERNITY" 1-13
Writers:	Tony Blake and Paul Jackson
Director:	Les Sheldon
Original airdate:	February 10, 1999
Guests:	Allen Cutler (Doug)
	Billy Drago (Demon)
	Jodie Hanson (Zoe)
	Kimberly Kates (Tanjella)
	Evan O'Meara (Richard Warner)
	Dailyn Matthews (Susan Warner)
	Steve Wilder (Lucas Devane)

REMEMBER WHEN . . .

. . . Prue's natural tendency to pooh-pooh superstitions, like a fear of Friday the thirteenth, was seriously undercut by an entry in their mother's handwriting, suggesting a fear demon really did stalk witches on that date. Unfortunately, Patty Halliwell didn't leave specific instructions on how to get rid of him, and her children had plenty of fear for him to feed on.

MAGICAL NOTES

A number of amulets, charms, and talismans crop up on *Charmed*, but as evidenced by Phoebe's willingness to put out good cash—even someone else's cash—on her lucky token, the Halliwells at this point obviously haven't tumbled on to the notion that they can create their own.

A common form of amulet is one for luck or protection and is achieved by symbolically compressing a spell into a single rune or image. Start by writing out exactly what you desire. Use an entire page, if you like. Then condense that wish to a single line. Then to a single word. Then to a single mark that represents all that went before. Burn the papers and collect the soot. Either enclose the soot in a locket or other item; or, alternatively, scatter the ashes and inscribe the last symbol on an object of your choice. Voilà.

TITLE	"SECRETS AND GUYS" 1-14
Teleplay by:	Constance M. Burge and Sheryl J. Anderson
Story by:	Brad Kern and Constance M. Burge
Director:	James A. Contner
Original airdate:	February 17, 1999
Guests:	Michael Bunin (Security guard)
	Richard Cody (Harry)
	Robert Gossett (Gordon Franklin)
	Brian Krause (Leo Wyatt)
	David Netter (Max Franklin)
	Will Stewart (David)
	Brad Tatum (Mickey Jackson)

REMEMBER WHEN . . .

. . .The spirit board got active, capturing the magical distress signal of a young boy named Max who happened to be a witch with telekinetic abilities similar to Prue's? As the sisters attempted to rescue him, Leo Wyatt's role as a defender of good witches was inadvertently revealed to Phoebe, leaving her wondering just how much sisters should be expected to share.

MAGICAL NOTES

The belief in entities whose special province is the protection of particular people is present in a surprising number of cultures, whether they call them white-lighters or guardian angels. Also surprising is the almost universal method of attracting such an entity: candle calling. In a quiet place, light a candle and hold it between your hands—be careful not to let hot wax splash your skin. Let it burn as you envision yourself wrapped in the embrace of a benevolent spirit. When you feel the warmth of the candle's flame inside yourself, blow out the candle as you close your eyes. The first image to come into your thoughts, be it a face, an animal, or just a scene, will be the image that becomes your focus in the future. You can only hope your protector is as handsome as, and more available than, Brian Krause!

TITLE	"IS THERE A WOOGY IN THE HOUSE?" 1-15
Writers:	Chris Levinson and Zack Estrin
Director:	John T. Kretchmer
Original airdate:	February 24, 1999
Guests:	Shawn Christian (Josh)
	Richard McGonagle
	Michael Mantell
	Nancy Moonves (Professor Beth Whittlesey)

Jennifer Rhodes (Penny Halliwell [Grams])

Cristine Rose (Claire)

Tait Ruppert (Neighbor Joe)

REMEMBER WHEN...

...An earthquake splits the basement floor? Piper and Prue feared a gas leak; Phoebe's fear, seated in a childhood terror enacted in this same house, was much more demonic—and much more immediate.

MAGICAL NOTES

Though several episodes hint that Halliwell Manor, the house itself, is an active magical entity, this episode spells that out most clearly. In the *Charmed* world, this power is explained by an accident of geography, but other magical circles would assume it to be a side effect of having generations of witches living there.

That items, even houses, pick up residual energy and magic is a long-established tenet. It rationalizes otherwise inexplicable effects, like haunting or auras, the reasons for keeping divinatory tools well insulated from the everyday world, and why certain objects seem more comfortable (for lack of a better word) than others used for the same purpose. Places, logically, are no different than objects, and several lines of magical thought include the concept of a homestead or covenstead, a place made special by the inhabitation of witches working for the common good.

TITLE   "WHICH PRUE IS IT ANYWAY?" 1-16

Writer: Javier Grillo-Marxuach

Director: John Benring

Original airdate: March 3, 1999

Guests: Mongo Brownlee (Luther Stubbs)

                  Susan Chuang (Monique)

Bernie Kopell (Coroner)

Alex MacArthur (Gabriel)

Cristine Rose (Claire)

Shannon Sturges (Helena Statler)

REMEMBER WHEN...

...After Phoebe received a terrifying vision of Prue being impaled on a crystal sword, she decides to attempt a spell to multiply her power. Instead, the girls found themselves confronted by three whole Prues, each of whom seemed bent on being the boss.

MAGICAL NOTES

Phoebe's visions of the future beg the simple question: Is it destiny, or can it all be changed? That question carries over into real-world practices like divination and astrology. For most practitioners, the future is seen as a series of possibilities emanating from points of decision or particular events. Few believe in an immutable series of actions, choosing instead to believe that humans can create their own destiny—with sufficient attention and work.

What purpose is there, then, in the divinatory arts? If nothing is set in stone, is true prophecy possible?

TITLE	"THAT '70S EPISODE" 1-17
Writer:	Sheryl J. Anderson
Director:	Richard Compton
Original airdate:	April 7, 1999
Guests:	Sally Ann Brooks (Officer at jail)
	Megan Corletto (Little Piper)
	Finola Hughes (Patti Halliwell)
	Andrew Jackson (Nicholas)
	Jennifer Rhodes (Penny Halliwell [Grams])
	Jake Sakson (Little Andy)
	Rey Silva (Police officer at park)
	Emmalee Thompson (Little Prue)

REMEMBER WHEN . . .

. . . A warlock appeared, claiming his invulverability to the sisters' powers resulted from a pact made with their mother? As the girls return to the 1970s to prevent the pact, emotions run high when they encounter not only their grandmother, and themselves as children, but their mother and a warlock all too ready to take full advantage of their understandably mixed feelings.

MAGICAL NOTES

One of the few episodes where we see witches living in a family setting and a variety of generations in an openly magical household, with younger ones learning from older. How different might a real child's younger years be in such a close-knit, supportive—and magical!—environment?

TITLE   "WHEN BAD WARLOCKS GO GOOD" 1-18

Writer:	Edithe Swenson
Director:	Kevin Inch
Original airdate:	April 28, 1999
Guests:	Frank Birney
	Stacie Chan (Little girl)
	Shawn Christian (Josh)
	Nick Kokotakis
	David Kriegel
	Dathan Hooper (Officer)
	Andrea E. Taylor (Girl victim)
	Michael Weatherly (Brendan Rowe)
	Anne Vareze (Nun)

REMEMBER WHEN . . .

. . . Prue's latest "innocent," a soon-to-be priest, turned out to be the third aspect of an Unholy Triangle, a sort of anti-Charmed Ones, the girls found themselves in a three-on-three match against a family with a history as long as their own; and who was determined to keep its youngest member from ever taking holy orders.

MAGICAL NOTES

The nature of warlocks gets fuzzier than ever in this episode—as does the nature of innate powers. Brendan claims that ordination will remove his powers, making it impossible for him to become a warlock. Yet, as Phoebe tells Prue and Piper in "Something Wicca This Way Comes," the girls were *born* witches. If warlocks are evil witches, and warlocks are initiated, why wasn't Brendan simply a witch to begin with? By the circumstances of this episode, a warlock would seem more like a demon than an evil witch.

TITLE	"BLIND SIDED" 1-19
Writers:	Tony Blake and Paul Jackson
Director:	Craig Zisk
Original airdate:	May 5, 1999
Guests:	Shawn Christian (Josh)
	Matt George (uncredited roles)
	Dennis Keiffer (Grimlock 2)
	Maureen Muldoon (Dee)
	Michael O'Connor (Jerry Cartwright)
	Scott Plank (Eric Lohman)
	Lucy Rodriguez (Housekeeper)
	Raphael Sbarge (uncredited roles)
	Scott Terra (David)

REMEMBER WHEN . . .

. . . In trying to prevent two children from being kidnapped from a public park, Prue inadvertently revealed her powers to a tabloid journalist? While Prue and Piper ducked the reporter to get hard proof of their active powers, Phoebe tracked down another victim who, twenty years earlier, had been returned, blind, from his encounter with the "sewer monsters."

MAGICAL NOTES

Auras, a metaphysical extension of living bodies, have been the subject of both arcane and scientific study. Psychics' claims, to be able to perceive a light of various colors surrounding people, and to deduce something of that person's characteristics and health from those colors, remain difficult to quantitatively investigate. Some people, like Amanda Rutledge, seem incredibly "lucky" in "guessing" the illnesses afflicting people she has never met before. Others seem completely unable to replicate her results. Kirilian photography, which has shown both sides of a leaf even after the leaf was cut in two, was seen by some as a bridge between metaphysical and physical sciences, though much work will still be required before even Kirilian photography moves into mainline scientific inquiry.

TITLE	"THE POWER OF TWO" ("THE GHOST OF ALCATRAZ") 1-20
Writer:	Brad Kern
Director:	Elodie Keene
Original airdate:	May 12, 1999
Guests:	Brenda Bakke (Soul collector)
	Don Brunner (Inspector Anderson)
	Susan Chuang (Monique)
	Jack Donner (Judge Renault)
	Victoria Fang (Marianne)
	Carlos Gomez (Inspector Rodriguez)
	Jim Hanna (CSI detective)
	Michelle Harrell (Inspector Blakely)
	Yuji Hasegawa (Mr. Yakihama)
	Sean Hennigan (Alcatraz guide)
	Jeff Kober (Jackson Ward)
	Gregg Monk (Officer)
	C(h)ristine Rose (Claire)
	Lesley Woods (Iris Beiderman)

REMEMBER WHEN . . .

. . . Phoebe watched the spirit of serial killer Jackson Ward hop a ride off Alcatraz in the body of a very recently deceased guard? Not only must she and Prue keep Piper in the dark about their latest bizarre quest—to prevent the ghost from killing everyone associated with his murder trial—but keep Andy Trudeau and Darryl Morris out of harm's way as well.

MAGICAL NOTES

That Jackson Ward, a spirit, can't travel over water fits with all the established folklore. If the Halliwell women had known the rest of that lore, they might have had an easier time dealing with their murderous ghost. Traditionally, a spirit can't cross a circle of salt, roses, or vervain, either, which means they could have at least contained him until the banishment could be handled under safer conditions.

TITLE	"LOVE HURTS" 1-21
Writers:	Chris Levinson, Zack Estrin, and Javier Grillo-Marxuach
Director:	James Whitmore
Original airdate:	May 19, 1999
Guests:	Con Brunner (Inspector Anderson)
	Carlos Gomez (Inspector Rodriguez)
	Lisa Robin Kelly (Daisy)
	Brian Krause (Leo Wyatt)
	Michael Trucco (Dark-lighter)
	Tom Yi (Hotel manager)

REMEMBER WHEN . . .

. . . The sisters' holiday plans were canceled at the reappearance of an injured, probably dying Leo Wyatt who begged them to protect Daisy, a young woman pursued by a dark-lighter? Even a spell-triggered exchange of powers, which Piper hoped would lend her Leo's ability to heal, may not be enough to save Leo or the next potential white-lighter.

MAGICAL NOTES

The spell obviously included more people than Piper intended to affect. After watching the setup for this spell—or rather, the lack of preparation—what do you think might be done differently to prevent such accidents in the future?

TITLE	"DÉJÀ VU ALL OVER AGAIN" 1-22
Writers:	Brad Kern and Constance M. Burge
Director:	Les Sheldon
Original airdate:	May 26, 1999
Guests:	Wendy Benson (Joanne Hertz)
	David Carradine (Tempus)
	Carlos Gomez (Inspector Rodriguez)
	Nancy O'Dell (Weatherperson)

REMEMBER WHEN...

...After killing his partner and attempting to frame Andy Trudeau for the crime, demon cum SFPD Inspector Rodriguez got a little extra help from a warlock with a knack for turning time back on itself? Only Phoebe's innate sense of past, present, and future gave the sisters any hope of ending the cycle and, finally, ending Rodriguez's homicidal attacks.

MAGICAL NOTES

Kit's alleged ability to spot evil demons isn't entirely rooted in either Wicca or witchcraft. The belief that cats and dogs could see fairies dates back to the last turn of the millennium in Ireland, with cats being noted for a dislike of the magical folk.

TITLE   "WITCH TRIAL" 2-01

Writer: Brad Kern

Director: Craig Zisk

Original airdate: September 20, 1999

Guests: Greg Cromer (Rob)

                  Rick Cramer (Nicholas)

                  Matt Entriken (Assistant)

                  Jesse Goins (Doctor)

                  Mark Hearing (Paramedic)

                  Walter Phelan (Abraxas)

                  Jennifer Rhodes (Penny Halliwell/Grams)

                  Janet Wood (Mrs. Milton)

REMEMBER WHEN . . .

. . . Abraxas, a demon from another plane, stole the *Book of Shadows* and the sisters were inundated with demons they'd thought already vanquished? Prue's mixed emotions about her powers and their role in Andy Trudeau's death threatened to leave the sisters divided, unable either to retrieve the book or banish Abraxas.

MAGICAL NOTES

Initiation is a ritual consistent with both Wicca and witchcraft traditions, but while Wicca recognizes both self-initiation and initiation through coven-based ritual, witchcraft tends to recognize only the group rituals of initiation. The self-initiation rites, which would include Phoebe's first casting of the Power of Three spell, would be regarded as a simple dedication without the binding oaths of a more formal group rite.

A simple ritual, acceptable as an initiation among most Wiccans and a initial dedication in other groups, is enacted inside a protective circle. After a period of meditation, the postulant goes though the following incantation three times:

In this circle, rightly drawn,
Knowledge is sought,
Truth be found.

In this circle, of the art,
A promise is given,
Oath of the heart.

In this circle, a magic seal,
A mind is open,
A soul to heal.

TITLE   "MORALITY BITES" 2-02

Writers: Chris Levinson and Zack Estrin
Director: John Behring
Original airdate: October 7, 1999
Guests: Michael Brownlee (Sports reporter)
                  Lisa Connaughton (Anne)
                  Claudia Gold (Screaming woman)
                  Jennifer Hale (Neighbor)
                  Dan Horton (Cal Greene)
                  Darron Johnson (Prison hallway guard)
                  Brian Krause (Leo Wyatt)
                  Richard Saxton (2009 news anchor)
                  Pat Skipper (Nathanial Pratt)
                  Taili Song (Assistant #2)
                  Clara Thomas (Melinda)
                  Tina Thomas (Assistant #1)
                  Sibila Vargas (Sierra Stone)

REMEMBER WHEN . . .

. . . Phoebe's premonitions took a horrific turn when she saw herself being burned to death for witchcraft? Traveling forward to

the future, the sisters discovered their lives were nothing like they expected—or hoped—and even the future Phoebe saw no way to avert her fate.

MAGICAL NOTES

Despite the supposed fate of Melinda Warren in *Charmed*'s fictional colonial period, and the pyre awaiting Phoebe in *Charmed*'s future, in America's real Salem trials, the women and men convicted of witchcraft were hanged. One was pressed to death; none were burned. Even in Europe, where many more were convicted, burning wasn't always the death of choice. The public spectacle depicted in this episode, however, faithfully reflects the circus feeling that often surrounded such executions.

TITLE	"THE PAINTED WORLD" 2-03
Writer:	Constance M. Burge
Director:	Kevin Inch
Original airdate:	October 14, 1999
Guests:	Anthony Deane (Applicant #1)
	Holly Fields (Jane)
	Rebecca Jackson (Applicant #2)
	Paul Kersey (Malcolm)
	Cindy Lu (Receptionist)
	Damian Perkins (Joe)
	Tate Taylor (Applicant #3)

REMEMBER WHEN...

...After a young woman brought an unusual painting of a castle to Prue at Buckland's for appraisal and sale, Prue discovered a man living inside the painting? A hidden message, revealed by routine X-ray examination of the picture, pulled first Prue, then Piper, inside, trapping them and leaving everybody's fate in Phoebe's already occupied hands.

MAGICAL NOTES

A little knowledge is a dangerous thing—as Phoebe realizes when her smart spell runs out of time. Real witches expect knowledge to come slowly, after considerable study. One modern school of witchcraft actually refuses to admit members who haven't already completed a degree program in both classics (including Latin and Greek) and theology! If that seems extreme, consider the tai chi master in Japan who refuses to acknowledge students who haven't already attended his open sunrise classes—without missing a single session—for five years!

TITLE   "THE DEVIL'S MUSIC" 2-04

Writer:	David Simkins
Director:	Richard Compton
Original airdate:	October 21, 1999
Guests:	Dishwalla (Dishwalla)
	Ralph Garman (DJ)
	David Haydn-Jones (Chris Barker)
	Larry Holden (Jeff Carlton)
	Brian Krause (Leo Wyatt)
	Robert Madrid (Roadie #1)
	Chris Nelson (Masselin)
	Alexandra Picatto (Tina Hitchens)
	Smalls (Bouncer)

REMEMBER WHEN...

...Piper's new—and so far obscure—club, P3, was about to get a social boost from the live appearance of the hot band Dishwalla? Leo's arrival to inform them that, far from the lucky break they'd hoped this to be, they would, in fact, spend this important evening tracking demons in the band's dressing room, quickly turned from simply unexpected to unwelcome and unappreciated.

MAGICAL NOTES

A nice reversal of the old stereotype that a *witch's* power comes from a deal with the devil, this episode does, however, continue a long history of pacts-with-evil-powers tales (*The Devil and Max Devlin* and *Ladyhawke*, for cinematic examples) that, of course, are actually morality plays warning sinners away from sin. Interestingly, neither Wicca nor witchcraft follow such literary precedents, instead encouraging their members to highly contemplative lives which includes vigorous, regular evaluation of the conscience.

TITLE	**"SHE'S A MAN, BABY, A MAN!"** 2-05
Writer:	Javier Grillo-Marxuach
Director:	Martha Mitchell
Original airdate:	November 4, 1999
Guests:	The Cranberries (The Cranberries)
	Georgia Emelin (Jan)
	Ralph Garman (DJ)
	Dean Kelly (Gorgeous man)
	Heidi Mark (Daria/The Succubus)
	Michael McLafferty (Dr. Owen Grant)
	Lex Medlin (Alan Stanton)
	Nick Stabile (Inspector Smith)
	Jamison Yang (Coroner)

REMEMBER WHEN...

...The heat wave covering San Francisco seems cool beside Phoebe's X-rated dreams? Prue's spell, cast to catch a man-killing succubus, had unexpected side effects that left Phoebe and Piper with a brother instead of a sister!

MAGICAL NOTES

Although much has been made of the sexual nature of succubi and incubi, the original models probably weren't physical manifestations at all. The practice of spending a night in contemplation of a deity within its temple was once fairly common; the aim, to have the deity manifest within the individual, was well accepted as not only possible but desirable. This spiritual entity's invasion of the body led to the word "incubi," to describe the person hosting the deity, not the deity itself.

TITLE   "THAT OLD BLACK MAGIC" 2-06

Writers: Vivian Mayhew and Valerie Mayhew
Director: James L. Conway
Original airdate: November 11, 1999
Guests: Liv Boughn (Heather)
                   Brigid Brannagh (Tuatha)
                   Jay Michael Ferguson (Kyle Gwydion)
                   John Johnston (Joshua)
                   Pamela Kosh (Betty)
                   Brian Krause (Leo Wyatt)
                   Teddy Lane, Jr. (Director)
                   Lochlyn Munro (Jack Sheridan)
                   Maulik Pancholy (Treasure hunter #1)
                   Jeremy Rowley (Treasure hunter #2)
                   Matthew Senko (Michael)

REMEMBER WHEN . . .

. . . The evil witch Tuatha was accidentally freed from her cave prison? Leo and the Charmed Ones must convince a very mortal, very insecure teenager named Kyle that he is, in fact, the Chosen One destined to destroy Tuatha's magical wand—preferably before Tuatha kills him.

MAGICAL NOTES

Though this episode gave the name "Tuatha" to a witch, it has other arcane connotations. In Celtic lore, the Tuatha de Damnu, also known as the Tuatha de Danaan, were a race of people who inhabited the world before human beings. Magical ability separated the races more so than appearance and, if the legend were true, then the Second Sight, dreams, and déjà vu would all be modern manifestations of an ancient interbreeding between the Tuatha de Danaan and humanity.

TITLE "THEY'RE EVERYWHERE" 2-07

Writer: Sheryl L. Anderson

Director: Mel Damski

Original airdate: November 18, 1999

Guests: Jim Antonio (Collector #2)

Misha Collins (Eric Bragg)

Lochlyn Munroe (Jack/Jeff Sheridan)

Dean Norris (Ben Bragg)

Eddy Saad (Dr. Stone/Collector 1)

Marcelo Tubert (Museum tour guide)

REMEMBER WHEN...

...Warlock paranoia broke out at Halliwell Manor after Prue saw her latest beau, Jack Sheridan, blink; Kit started hissing at Piper's guy, Dan; and Phoebe's premonition, brought on by contact with Eric, a young man who's caught her eyes, showed a brain-sucking warlock attacking him. What would be higher on the To-Contend-With-Today list? Only imminent destruction of the world, that's all.

MAGICAL NOTES

The *Charmed* universe turned the tables in this episode, making a historic method of witch detection, pricking, into a way for witches to identify warlocks. If the same trick holds true for other ways of discovering a witch, they'll also be able to check future boyfriends for witch's teats, skin discolorations from which a witch supposedly fed her familiar; the Touch, an insensitivity to pain; or the small lock of white hair found somewhere on a witch's body.

TITLE   "P3 H2O" 2-08

Writers: Chris Levinson and Zack Estrin
Director: John Behring
Original airdate: December 9, 1999
Guests: Ferrell Barron (Medic)
                    Pat Crowley (Mrs. Johnson)
                    Finola Hughes (Patty Halliwell)
                    Scott Jaeck (Sam Wilder)
                    Lucky Luciano (Kid #1)
                    Brian Krause (Leo Wyatt)
                    Lochlyn Munro (Jack Sheridan)
                    Emmalee Thompson (Young Prue)

REMEMBER WHEN...

...A man drowned before Prue's eyes, at their old summer camp, in the same lake where her mother died? Older, more schooled in the magical possibilities, the sisters determine that their mother's death wasn't a simple water accident, that there's a demon still inhabiting the lake, one who must be vanquished before it can take more lives.

MAGICAL NOTES

Unique from a magical standpoint, this episode demonstrates a banishment accomplished not through spells or innate powers, but by old-fashioned physics. Perhaps this is a good time to pause and remember the first rule of magic: Not every problem has, or requires, a magical solution. Part of the preparation for every spell should be reflection on the more mundane options available for resolving difficulties.

TITLE   "MS. HELLFIRE" 2-09

Teleplay by: Constance M. Burge and Sheryl J. Anderson
Story by: Constance M. Burge
Director: Craig Zisk

Original airdate:	January 13, 2000
Guests:	Carlo Castronovo (Willis)
	Billy Drago (Barbas)
	Courtney Gains (Marcie Steadwell)
	Lochlyn Munro (Jack Sheridan)
	Antonio Sabato, Jr. (Bane)
	Tom Simmons (Coroner)
	Hynden Walch (DJ)

REMEMBER WHEN...

...Ms. Hellfire, a hitwoman with great closets, has targeted the Halliwells? Prue's momentary self-indulgence as a clotheshorse for Ms. Hellfire's substantial wardrobe led to her being mistaken for the killer, a role she continued to play in hopes of locating Ms. Hellfire's boss.

MAGICAL NOTES

During the medieval period, it was believed that fears, like demons or illness, entered through an unwary mouth. Gossipy women were frowned upon, while "wise" women held their peace and learned by watching. Even if the so-called wise women of that period weren't witches in the sense we understand them today, there's still a lot to be said for taking the time to be observant, to think before speaking, and to keeping your ears open.

TITLE   "HEARTBREAK CITY" 2-10

Writer:	David Simkins
Director:	Michael Zinberg
Original airdate:	January 20, 2000
Guests:	Jonathan Aubé (Kevin)
	Michael Reilly Burke (Cupid)
	Brody Hutzler (Max)
	Lochlyn Munro (Jack Sheridan)
	Clayton Rohner (Drazi)
	Tiffany Salerno (Cindy)

REMEMBER WHEN...

...In the midst of a group outing where Phoebe was the only person dateless, a injured Cupid arrived seeking help and claiming that his evil counterpart, Drazi, was about to tear apart all the love Cupid had put together? Unless Phoebe could open her heart, even the Charmed Ones' pairings were endangered.

MAGICAL NOTES

Sometimes love doesn't need anything dramatic—or melodramatic—to make it better, just a renewal. Unlike most love spells, which could be considered as impinging on another's will, this one is a spell for two, to help remember all those things that brought a couple together in the first place.

A Spell to Restore Love

> Let Magic work Here,
> Between and Amongst Us.
> Repair our Hearts,
> Renew our Souls,
> Recall dear Memories,
> Rekindle the Love.

Of course, the accoutrements for this spell, namely two skyclad participants, a warm fire, two glasses of spiced wine, and red ribbons and candles, couldn't really hurt a relationship, could they?

TITLE	"RECKLESS ABANDON" 2-11
Writer:	Javier Grillo-Marxuach
Director:	Craig Zisk
Original airdate:	January 27, 2000
Guests:	Stephanie Beacham (Martha van Lewen)

J. Kenneth Campbell (Elias Lundy)
Ric Coy (Gilbert van Lewen)
Hillary Danner (Alexandra van Lewen)
Rolando Molina (Hernandez)
Lochlyn Munro (Jack Sheridan)
Albert Stroth (Uniformed cop)

REMEMBER WHEN . . .

. . . Phoebe encountered an abandoned baby in the police station? Once in contact with the little boy, Phoebe received a vision of the child's father attempting to kidnap the boy from their own home, a home haunted by a particularly deadly ghost.

MAGICAL NOTES

Within the Christian religions, suicide retains a nasty stigmata. That isn't true of either Wicca or witchcraft, perhaps because both religions encompass the concept of reincarnation, that we all get at least a second chance to correct our mistakes, do things differently. Occasionally, spirits do rest in the summerland before reembarking on the journey of discovery, but for most Wiccans, life *and* death are stops on the same learning curve.

TITLE	"AWAKENED" 2-12
Writers:	Vivian Mayhew and Valerie Mayhew
Director:	Anson Williams
Original airdate:	February 3, 2000
Guests:	Louisa Abernathy (Angie)
	Monica Allison (Nurse)
	Andrew Ducote (Nathan)
	Matthew Glave (Dr. Williamson)
	Lisa Ann Grant (Female reporter #2)
	Brian Krause (Leo Wyatt)

Jennifer Massey (Female reporter #1)

Lochlyn Munro (Jack Sheridan)

Daniel Reichert (Dr. Seigler)

Faith Salie (Second nurse)

Chuti Tiu (Asian-American nurse)

REMEMBER WHEN...

...A batch of fruit smuggled into the bar brought with it an Oroya Fever–infested sandfly, which bit Piper and sent her into a life-threatending coma? Nothing, not the *Book of Shadows*, not even Leo, seemed capable of preventing her death.

MAGICAL NOTES

That the Halliwells' *Book of Shadows* seems bereft of healing spells only emphasizes the differences between TV magic and real-world magic. While few Wiccans keep demon-bashing incantations in their books, few would be without basic healing spells. They certainly wouldn't have to muddle through with nothing more than an Awakening Spell. Many illness-specific spells exist, but wise modern witches do well to gather those directed at general health and the prevention of sickness.

TITLE   "ANIMAL PRAGMATISM" 2-13

Writers:	Chris Levinson and Zack Estrin
Director:	Don Kurt
Original airdate:	February 10, 2000
Guests:	Tim Griffin
	Benton Jennings (Concerned citizen)
	Katie Johnston
	Brian Krause (Leo Wyatt)
	Lela Lee
	Kelly McNair
	Steve Monroe
	Janice Robinson (Janice Robinson/herself)

Amber Skalski (Girl)

Rafer Weigel

Richard Wharton (Professor)

Christopher Wiehl

REMEMBER WHEN . . .

. . . Phoebe corrected a love spell from a magic book that three of her friends found in the campus bookstore on Valentine's Day, inadvertently making it possible for them to turn pets into dates? The new-made men, realizing they have a limited time in human form, immediately start hunting Phoebe, who they believe can make it permanent.

MAGICAL NOTES

As Phoebe points out at the beginning of this episode, there's a certain "grammar" to spellcasting. Just as rituals break down into well-defined parts like cleansing or grounding, formal or intricate spells follow a plan as well:

1. Evocation
2. Limitation
3. Purpose
4. Desire
5. Thanksgiving

TITLE	"PARDON MY PAST" 2-14
Writer:	Michael Gleason
Director:	Jon Paré
Original airdate:	February 17, 2000
Guests:	Daveigh Chase (Young Christina)
	Tyler Christopher (Anton)
	Lauri Hendler (Socialite)
	Gregg Kovan (Bouncer)
	Jeanette Miller (Christina Larson)
	Susan Savage (Classy Woman)

REMEMBER WHEN...

...An unseen assailant attempted to seduce Phoebe, prompting Leo to postulate that one of Phoebe's past lives was warning her of an ongoing danger? A spell takes her back to 1924, where she discovers her former self and a warlock were conspiring to steal the former Prue and Piper's powers—an act which would doom Phoebe to die on the anniversary of her past life's death.

MAGICAL NOTES

Past lives would be a natural consequence of reincarnation, a belief held by many Wiccans, so rituals designed to access those memories are fairly common. Several, in slightly longer form, resemble the incantation cast during this episode. What perspectives might a Wiccan gain by contacting a former self? Under what circumstances might a thinning of the wall between lives be detrimental?

TITLE   "GIVE ME A SIGN" 2-15

Writer: Sheryl J. Anderson
Director: James A. Contner
Original airdate: February 24, 1999
Guests: Keith Brunsmann (Litvack's henchman)
                   Janis Chow (Female newscaster)
                   Sean Christopher Davis (Delivery guy)
                   Anthony Holiday (Other guard)
                   Gwen McGee (TV anchor)
                   Geoff Meed (Guard #1)
                   Steve Railsback (Litvack)
                   Sal Rendino (Guard #2)
                   Antonio Sabato, Jr. (Bane Jessop)

REMEMBER WHEN...

...Bane Jessop, who once attempted to have the Charmed Ones killed, kidnapped Prue in hope of recruiting her help against Litvack, a mutual enemy? While Pheobe was looking for magical insight into Piper's love triangle, Prue found herself dealing with the more immediate, conflicting emotions for this intriguing, and handsome, young man.

MAGICAL NOTES

Several episodes dealt with the consequences of casting spells for personal gain, or casting spells to deliberately change another's feelings, but "Give Me a Sign" is the only episode to date questioning the morality of casting a spell *for* another person, but against that person's will. As it turns out, Phoebe's spell was poorly crafted in the first place—it could have applied as easily to Prue as to Piper—but considering how many red herrings sprang from Phoebe's spell, it's likely that, even in the *Charmed* universe, casting spells for another without consent is a no-no. What spells would you consider casting for someone else? In light of this episode, which of them might you reconsider? Is there a general rule you could create for yourself on this issue?

TITLE   **"MURPHY'S LUCK" 2-16**

Writer:	David Simkins
Director:	John Behring
Original airdate:	March 30, 2000
Guests:	Amy Adams (Maggie Murphy)
	Kent Faulcon (Mr. Corso)
	Arnold Vosloo (Dark-lighter)

REMEMBER WHEN...

...Prue stopped a dark-lighter's malicious interference in the life of Maggie Murphy, a future white-lighter, only to become the dark-lighter's new target? After surrounding Prue with bad luck, he began whispering doubts and fears in her mind, pushing her closer and closer to despair.

MAGICAL NOTES

Luck, in a magical sense, doesn't exist. Spells to increase one's luck, therefore, don't exist. Witchcraft requires a much more precise request, be it for wealth, love, health, or whatever.

What is interesting about this episode is its title, a reference to Murphy's Law (usually given as "Anything that can go wrong, will") which isn't actually attributable to Murphy, a real person. What Edward A. Murphy, Jr., actually said after all sixteen of the accelerometers on his experimental engine model were installed backward was "If there are two or more ways to do something, and one of those ways can result in a catastrophe, then someone will do it." The "Anything that can go wrong, will" version belongs to Larry Niven, whose character Finagle expressed this as "Finagle's Law of Dynamic Negatives."

TITLE	"HOW TO MAKE A QUILT OUT OF AMERICANS" 2-17
Teleplay by:	Javier Grillo-Marxuach and Robert Masello
Story by:	Javier Grillo-Marxuach
Director:	Kevin Inch
Original airdate:	April 6, 2000
Guests:	Cameron Bancroft (Cryto)
	Lucy Lee Flippin (Helen)
	Pamela Gordon (Amanda)
	John Gowans (Mr. York)
	Anne Haney (Gail Altman)
	Julia Lee (Young Gail)
	Charles C. Stevenson, Jr. (Caddie guy #2)
	Bill Wiley (Caddie guy #1)

REMEMBER WHEN . . .

. . . Aunt Gail turned up claiming that her community was threatened by Cryto, a demon who hands out youth and health in exchange for his victims' souls? The sisters' investigation leaves them powerless, a situation at least one of them hopes to continue indefinitely.

MAGICAL NOTES

At various times, each of the sisters has wished herself normal again. If you undertake the serious study of magic and ritual, you'll frequently be tempted to give up. It's a steep learning curve, requiring a wide range of interests, from history to folklore to psychology to languages to pharmacology. Then again, that explains why witches are some of the most interesting people you'll meet, and why friendships among those studying the arts so often do last a lifetime.

TITLE	"CHICK FLICK" 2-18
Writers:	Chris Levinson and Zack Estrin
Director:	Michael Schultz
Original airdate:	April 20, 2000
Guests:	August Amarino (Projectionist)
	Mark Lindsay Chapman (Finley Beck)
	Robin Atkin Downes (Demon of Illusion)
	Dale Fabrigar (Irritated guy)
	Kent Faulcon (Mr. Corso)
	Chris Payne Gilbert (Billy)
	Leslie Lauten (Sally Mae)
	Alec Ledd (Film geek)
	Michael Rivkin (Cell phone guy)
	J. P. Romano (The Slasher)
	Olivia Summers (Bloody Mary)

REMEMBER WHEN . . .

. . . A Demon of Illusion hiding in one of Phoebe's favorite movies started hopping between the real world and the film world, bringing the monsters of classic horror films into San Francisco with him? Only Phoebe's knowledge of all things B-rated can give the sisters time to vanquish this demon.

MAGICAL NOTES

When Prue asks Phoebe to cast a spell on the Illusion demon, in the middle of a theater, in front of witnesses, Phoebe's instinctive reaction is "We know nothing about the guy—I can't just whip one [a spell] up!" The rest of the episode goes on to prove that she should have gone with her gut.

Spontaneous magic seldom works without consequences on *Charmed,* a lesson that accurately reflects most real-world Wiccan belief. A 1956 manuscript provides this piece of sage advice to the young witch:

> When asked you are to give advice,
> Think you once—then think twice.
> If 'tis magic calls you to its side,
> In peace a full moon abide.
> What's made today can't be undone,
> Not in a full turning of the Sun.
> Mind night's first rule,
> Be you not another's fool.

TITLE	"EX LIBRIS" 2-19
Teleplay by:	Brad Kern
Story by:	Peter Chomsky
Director:	Joel J. Feigenbaum
Original airdate:	April 27, 2000
Guests:	Rebecca Cross (Charlene Hughes)
	Cleavant Derricks (Cleavant Wilson)
	Peg Stewart (Lillian)
	Jeremy Roberts (Gibbs)
	The Goo Goo Dolls (Themselves)

REMEMBER WHEN...

...One of Phoebe's college friends, decapitated because she was getting too close to proving that demons actually exist, turned up as a disembodied ghost who didn't know she was dead? It was up to the Halliwell witches to discover what the ghost still had to offer the living before they could avenge her death and let her spirit move on.

MAGICAL NOTES

Demons are a huge part of the *Charmed* lore, a situation *not* reflected in Wiccan belief. *The Complete Book of Devils and Demons* by Leonard R. N. Ashley, a real book found among Charlene's effects at the library, lists hundreds, if not thousands, of demons by name, gathered from scores of religions and mythologies. Believers in demons, regardless of their geographic locale, agree that taking on a demon is made much easier by knowing who and what type it is.

Some of those better known than the Libris demon of this episode are:

Beelzebub: Not the Christian devil but his aide, aka the Prince of Demons or Lord of the Flies.

Belphegor: Demon of Ingenius Discoveries and Wealth

Jezebeth: The Falsehood Demon, aka Woman of Lies

Leviathan: In Judeo-Christian demonology, the seducer of both Adam and Eve and First General of the Armies of Hell. This demon is neither male nor female and takes its victims equally from both sexes.

Murmur: The Demon of Music. Hopefully this Count of Hell, a sort of uber-demon, won't be a special musical guest at P3 any time in the near future.

Samael: Believed to be the serpent demon who tempted Eve, his door plaque is usually the Angel of Death, which just happens to reflect the most common real-world belief about the origin of demons, that they're fallen angels.

Several early Christian and Judaic writers believed that a finite number of demons were created all on a single night, the night Satan led a rebellion in Heaven and was cast out. According to that belief, no more demons can ever be created, so, each demon vanquished reduces the total number of evil servants out there fighting the forces of good. Good news for the Charmed Ones!

TITLE	"ASTRAL MONKEY" 2-20
Teleplay by:	Constance M. Burge and David Simkins
Story by:	Constance M. Burge
Director:	Craig Zisk
Original airdate:	May 4, 2000
Guests:	Jim Davidson (Evan Stone)
	Matthew Glave (Dr. Williamson)
	Deirdre Holder (Nurse #1)
	Karen James (Sally Dopler)
	Gary Douglas Kohn (Benny Ritter)
	Susan Martino (Lucy)
	Jack Maxwell (Barry)
	Lina Patel (Doctor #1)
	Milt Tarver (Dr. Jeffries)

REMEMBER WHEN...

...Doctor Williamson, who was stumped by Piper's impossible recovery from Oroya Fever, decided to inject lab monkeys with the Halliwell sisters' blood? Things might have been complicated, but still manageable, if he hadn't also been accidentally injected with the same blood and discovered, firsthand, exactly what power the sisters wield.

MAGICAL NOTES

Blood's esoteric and more practical aspects have intrigued human investigators since it was first spilled. Magical rites often acknowledge blood as near magical in its own right. In *Charmed*, the sisters call Melinda Warren into the present by an act of "blood calling to blood." Historically, it was believed that a witch's pact with the Devil was signed in blood. The genetic wizardry of modern times, linking criminals to crime scenes for example, would certainly appear magical to the Colonials, though, with their background of belief, associating blood with the soul, they might be more willing than a modern jury to believe that spilling blood at the scene of a crime would spiritually tie the perpetrator to the site, that the science of blood and its DNA can do the same thing. Witness the O.J. trial!

In either case, whether by magic or genetics, the notion that blood might be a carrier of special traits like the Halliwell's powers, is wholly consistent with humankind's long-standing beliefs and relationships with its own blood.

Of course, the precept of this episode, that injection with the Halliwell blood can transfer a magical power to another person—or animal—does raise some interesting possibilities for further episodes. If the monkeys all survived being given a single Halliwell power, it stands to reason that a person could as well. Does that mean they could create as many Threesomes as necessary to help combat evil?

TITLE   "APOCALYPSE, NOT" 2-21

Teleplay by:	Sheryl J. Anderson
Story by:	Sanford Golden
Director:	Michael Zinberg
Original airdate:	May 11, 2000
Guests:	Geoffrey Blake (Strife)
	Gannon Brown (Worker #1)
	Kenneth Cortland (Assistant)
	Peter Able Holden (Worker #2)
	Patrick Kilpatrick (Death)
	Keith Ramsey (Bartender)

Jeff Ricketts (Famine)
Brian Thompson (War)
The Paula Cole Band (Themselves)

REMEMBER WHEN...

...Piper and Phoebe found themselves joining forces with the dark side when Prue, along with one of the Four Horsemen of the Apocalypse, are sucked into a magical vortex created by the joint use of good and evil powers? Given a choice between saving a sister and saving the world, again, the remaining sisters find themselves wavering on the edge of the apocalypse.

MAGICAL NOTES

This isn't the Halliwells' first encounter with demons, or other planes of existence, but it's the first episode where any character has tried to quantify the demons, to rank the opposition the sisters have been fighting, to solidify the rather nebulous concepts that have formed the background for all the action on *Charmed*.

Leo identifies eleven ranks in the hierarchy they face.

Traditional mythology, that is to say traditional Christian demon mythology, probably ranked the demons that the common folk weren't supposed to really believe in as soon as they'd memorized the rankings of the angels preached to them from the pulpit, which is to say earlier than A.D. 900. Their neighbors had done the same thing considerably earlier. The Jews, Babylonians, and nearly everyone else with a written language all had elaborate systems and family trees to describe their demons before Christianity was born. Not surprisingly, Christians put their Satan at the top of the heap and ranked everyone else below him, with the hierarchy divided into Princes, Ministers, Ambassadors, Justices, The House of Princes, and Trivial Spirits. The ranks within the hierarchy are as follows:

Emperor—Satan, Lucifer

Prince of Hell—Beelzebub

Grand Duke—Astarot

Prime Ministers—Lucifere, et al

Grand Generals—Sanachias, et al

Lower Generals—Agalipta, et al

Lieutenant Generals—Methophites, et al

Brigadiers—Arithesis, et al

Marquis de Camp—Kamechias, et al

Count de Camp—Erebius, et al

The Horsemen would, in this scheme, be the rank of Grand Generals. Nasty.

TITLE	**"BE CAREFUL WHAT YOU WITCH FOR"** 2-22
Teleplay by:	Brad Kern, Zack Estrin, and Chris Levinson
Story by:	Brad Kern
Director:	Shannen Doherty
Original airdate:	May 18, 2000
Guests:	Jeff Corey
	Marcus Graham
	J. G. Hertzler
	Joshua Hutchinson (Dick)
	Zitto Kazann
	French Stewart (The Genie)

REMEMBER WHEN...

...A dragon demon and the Infernal Council turned a genie loose to tempt the Halliwells into revealing their deepest desires? As the Council hoped, wishes became weapons when one of those wishes threatened to undo the Power of Three.

MAGICAL NOTES

If genies seem a bit far afield from the usual collection of demons and warlocks, that's because the jinn, the djin, and their ilk are from Muslim demonology rather than the Judeo-Christian roots with which our literature and cinema are more likely to be imbued. In Spain, when Muslims and Christians lived in close proximity, the genies became integrated with tales of spirits caught in lamps, mirrors, and, of course, bottles.

Four thousand years ago, according to Muslim belief, a spirit named Iblis and his four sons dared to question God, so were turned to smoke and confined in a jar. One variation, the one made popular in Western culture, suggested that, unlike the Judeo-Christian variety of demon—which can't be redeemed by good works, contrition, or anything else—the genie could, by his acts of goodness, return to heaven.

Bloopers!

1-01 "SOMETHING WICCA THIS WAY COMES"
When, exactly...

...does Phoebe have time to read all that stuff about "timing, feeling, and the phases of the moon"? She opens the book to the first page, reads the title, turns to the second page, reads the incantation, and the other two sisters arrive! Is she speed-reading the index in the four seconds it takes for the sparkly special effect in the chandelier?

...does the tree in front of the Halliwell house have time to bloom? The night the sisters receive their powers, Jeremy walks under the tree, which is absolutely bare of bloom or leaf. Yet the next morning, a scant six or seven hours later, the same tree is in full leaf!

...does Piper impale her poppet with the rose—before or after reciting the verbal component of the spell? If you watch this episode, it seems she does it *twice*, both before *and* after the spell.

For your further contemplation:

If the Halliwell sisters are burning those candles in the attic, why aren't the wicks burned when they clean up?

If the elevator is going up, up, up while Jeremy attacks Piper, how does he end up crawling over the same stack of wooden pallets, to leave by a doorway that should have been many floors below them?

1-02 "I'VE GOT YOU UNDER MY SKIN"
Did you find any?

1-03 "THANK YOU FOR NOT MORPHING"
If all three shape-shifters are *inside* when the girls arrive at the house party, who is the shape-shifted dog *outside*, watching them arrive?

Flames are never easy items to manage on sets. Candles burn down quickly and give away the time between takes, requiring artificial flames to be set up in some scenes. Logs roll about inside fireplaces. In this episode, a flambéed dessert continues to burn away even after Piper freezes the entire kitchen.

During Phoebe's first trip to the attic in this episode, the *Book of Shadows* does its self-flipping thing, revealing that many pages were actually doubles of previous pages!

For your further consideration:

When confronted by the dog in her house, why doesn't Prue (a) physically close the door between her and the dog as she was leaving; or (b) mentally "move" the dog out of the open door? For that matter, when Phoebe locks Prudence on the far side of the door, why doesn't she just turn the knob with her mind? She doesn't hesitate to use her power to "push" the book under the stand, but wouldn't she use it when threatened by all that drool and teeth?

Who set the attic door on edge? When it is first kicked out of its frame, doesn't it just fall flat for the shape-shifter to walk in?

1-04 "DEAD MAN DATING"

Two contradictory sets of images resulting from two-camera setups arise in "Dead Man Dating": Early in the episode, we watch from a front-facing setup as Piper finishes gathering up party invitations; yet from the reverse angle, which comes next, she is just beginning the same task. In the later sequences, a reverse shot shows the villain with a gun held to Piper's neck; the front-facing shot, however, dangles that same gun harmlessly by his side.

A related set of bloopers arises from a different sort of two-setup scenario; whenever Piper freezes time, a before-and-after scenario is in effect, which occasionally results in some odd discontinuity. For example, during this episode, Piper freezes the scene after Tony shoots at Prue. In the postfreeze scene, a quick head count reveals several fewer heads than in the prefreeze scene.

For your further consideration:

Mark can sit on furniture, but he can't turn on the TV, knock on or open the door, or stop a flying cup. He can sit in Piper's car—it doesn't go off and leave him—but the bicycle messenger goes right through him. So why does Piper risk looking insane by holding open the car door for an invisible man?

How is Mark, six inches taller than Tony, supposed to make a believable corpse substitute?

1-05 "DREAM SORCERER"

In the dream, Prue's left shoulder is scratched, yet when she gets out of the tub, it's her right shoulder that's injured.

For your further consideration:

How did Piper, standing directly behind Prue, *not* see those big ugly scratches on her sister's back?

1-06 "THE WEDDING FROM HELL"

What's with Prue's purse? In the final confrontation with the demon bride, Prue looks in her purse for the poniard—the same purse Elliot picks up off the floor, and the purse we see once again in Prue's hands even while Elliot is rummaging through it!

That isn't the only purse appearing and disappearing in this episode. Watch as events unfold just before and just after the alarm sounds. Not only does Phoebe's purse show up at random, so does her jacket!

For your further consideration:

How long does it take the SFPD to respond to a dead-priest-in-the-driveway call-out, anyway? At least long enough for Jade d'Mon to change out of a wedding dress and into a cute sweater set?

About that "protect the innocent" thing—was the stripper not innocent enough?

1-07 "THE FOURTH SISTER"

"Mirrors never lie," Aviva tells Phoebe, but they do, especially when Kali appears in the mirror in Phoebe's bedroom. Although Phoebe is actually in bed at night, the reflection in the mirror shows a daylight scene with the bed neatly made and absolutely no sign of Phoebe! Again, in Aviva's room, when Prue opens the closet door, the reflection in the mirror shows Prue standing in front of a closed door, not an open closet.

A local resident who doesn't like *Charmed* filming in his nice Victorian neighborhood is so determined to make life difficult for the location crew that he's been known to bang pots and pans together to spoil their sound!

For your further consideration:

How does Aviva's sweater, which is left in the conservatory, end up on the back of a chair in the kitchen, a nice convenient location for Phoebe to pick it up?

What happens to the burning hatbox and dressmaker's model?

They turn up in future episodes—unscathed!

While you're watching for minutiae, take this opportunity to note the address on the flyers Leo posts around town: 7571 Prescott Street, right?

1-08 "THE TRUTH IS OUT THERE... AND IT HURTS"
Did you find any?

1-09 "THE WITCH IS BACK"
Luckily for passersby outside Prue's office, the glass that should have rained down on them when Matthew broke her window conveniently disappears before reaching the ground, where it should have been visible during the overhead camera shots.

1-10 "WICCA ENVY"
Another prefreeze/postfreeze blooper in this episode: Prefreeze, Leo leans on the doorframe; postfreeze, he isn't.

1-11 "FEATS OF CLAY"
Did you find any?

1-12 "THE WENDIGO"
The Incredible Hulk should have been a guide to anyone producing an episode like this one; it certainly included all the bloopers common on that old series. First of all, when Piper turns wendigo in the attic, what happens to her clothes? We see them ripping off, but they've disappeared in the long shot that follows, revealing the floor. When the wendigo ripped someone else's shirt, namely Andy's, the material is shown in its open con-

dition in one shot, but perfectly neat in the one immediately following! Keeping a tidy set is, no doubt, a virtue, but, if you're going to shred fabric, you've just got to leave a little material lying about!

For your further consideration:

Why does Andy, who has known the girls all his life, suddenly not know which sister was which when he introduces the Halliwells to Agent Fallon?

Doesn't Prue show an inordinate accuracy with that flare gun—for trees?

1-13 "FROM FEAR TO ETERNITY"

For your further consideration:

Why would anyone like Tanjella, whose greatest fear is being buried alive in an earthquake, live in San Francisco in the first place?

Among fans, this episode will likely be remembered as "What's with That Hair/Clothes/Water, Anyway?"

1. How does Prue get her hair dried and styled between her dunking in the pool and her house?
2. How does Andy, a trained investigator, not spot the new white streak in Prue's hair when she was in the shower? (Of course, viewers aren't supposed to spot that huge patch of makeup covering Shannen Doherty's real-life tattoo either, right?) If the white streak is there for Phoebe to see so plainly, what happens to it in later shots? Another mysterious midnight run to the hairdresser?

What's really puzzling is how, after all the toiletry bottles are floating about in the shower with Prue, they're all neatly lined up again when Andy arrives! Who'd have thought Prue was so tidy, so domestically inclined, especially while trying to avoid drowning?

While everyone recognizes that San Francisco is in California, a nice warm state, water seems to evaporate faster there than anywhere else! When water is spilled on Phoebe's dress, it immediately disappears.

No episode would be complete without a wardrobe blooper. While Prue is floating about in the pool, her bra strap is visible, her *white* bra strap; when she gets out of the pool, her bra strap is still visible, her *black* bra strap.

The prop blooper of this episode, however, definitely belongs to Phoebe's good-luck coin, which disappears completely in mid-scene!

1-14 "SECRETS AND GUYS"

Even in water glasses filled by magical means, ice floats.

For your further consideration:

Supposing Phoebe hadn't seen him hovering around the chandelier, how would Leo explain repairing the fixture with nary a ladder nor chair in sight?

If she believes she's discovered a warlock dangling from her ceiling, why does Phoebe hang up on Piper instead of screaming for help?

Why can a kid who opens electrical panels at a distance not undo a few knots right in front of himself? Psychokinesis may be an ability to move things you *can't* see, but why would that prevent your moving things you *can* see? Or, if it did, why not just close your eyes? For that matter, if Max can override the electrical circuitry of the alarms, why not the circuitry of the detonator *before* they get to the bank?

1-15 "IS THERE A WOOGY IN THE HOUSE?"

Although Kit the cat streaks out of the house with no collar, the collar is back in place when she returns!

For your further consideration:

Would a gas-line repairman really flick on the basement lights *before* eliminating the possibility of a gas leak?

1329 Prescott Street? Is Phoebe having her pizza delivered to her house or the neighbors'? In "The Fourth Sister," the lost-cat flyers for Kit gave a different address, remember? In a show where magic is always a possibility, "moving house" sure gets a whole new meaning.

Shanda Lear? Perhaps the writers weren't aware of it, but there really is a famous Shanda Lear: She's the daughter of the Lears famous for executive jets! Or maybe they did know....

If you've been wondering about the appearing and disappearing tattoos, this episode gives you the opportunity to spot one of Alyssa Milano's, one that's covered with body makeup for most other occasions.

Other objects appearing and disappearing in this episode include the water from a toppled vase, the same *broken* vase that mysteriously turns up whole.

Although we've seen numerous scenes in the Halliwell kitchen, this is the only episode when Grams's picture is seen anywhere in the room, much less in the oh-so-convenient spot next to the basement door.

Bloopers can slip in from any number of sources, often as the result of having scenes or lines cut in the interest of time. In this episode, Piper *knows* Phoebe is in the basement, despite the fact that the only other character who could possibly know that, the gasman, didn't pass along that information.

1-16 "WHICH PRUE IS IT ANYWAY?"

If Gabriel was alive at the time of the Halliwell sisters' ancestor Briana and, as claimed, his sister, Helena, was a "living, breathing" person, how was Helena alive in our time?

More hair bloopers! Watch Piper's hair go from down-do to ponytail as she races upstairs to the attic. Neat trick, that, for the witch on the go.

For your further consideration:

What happens to the statue after this episode?

1-17 "THAT '70S EPISODE"

If there's one thing Hollywood is *not* short of, it's extras, which makes it hard to justify having the same couple both leaving Buddies and, concurrently, sitting at a table in the middle of the scene.

As no episode is complete without a prop blooper, ask yourself where the key holder that was in the kitchen back in the '70s went while Penny Halliwell is talking on the phone.

1-18 "WHEN BAD WARLOCKS GO GOOD"

For your further consideration:

If ordination, in and of itself, is enough to keep Brendon "safe," why isn't Father Austin safe? If entering holy orders is protection against warlocks and demons, then no one should have been thrown through the window at the Spencer estate in "The Wedding from Hell," either. Obviously, "safe" has a different meaning for warlocks than the rest of us!

1-19 "BLIND SIDED"

In this episode, a reporter looks for bloopers on his videotape. Bet you he would have caught these bloopers during this episode....

Where do the trees go after the Grimlock and David go through the hole in the ground? Despite being in a fairly close copse of trees at the beginning of the scene, Prue is standing at the edge of a meadow after the two disappear.

Who pours up the potion while Prue is on the phone with Phoebe?

Some bloopers occur so regularly they could be incorporated into some fun drinking or party games. In this episode, there's another disappearing accessory. Watch Phoebe's purse appear, disappear, and reappear as she discovers the drain entrance.

1-20 "THE POWER OF TWO"

About that dressmaker's bust in the attic this episode—it's looking good for an item that caught fire in "The Fourth Sister."

For your further consideration:

Those windows in the attic, the one with the curved top opposite the doorway and the stained-glass porthole window on the wall to the right as you enter the attic—why aren't they visible on the outside of the house? We've seen three sides of the house up to now and, as those attic windows are on different walls, not seeing them from the outside would have been impossible.

Prop bloopers really get a chuckle in "The Power of Two." During the climatic scene, Prue downs the entire glass of death potion in good Socratic style; yet, when next we see the glass, there's still red concoction in it.

1-21 "LOVE HURTS"

Did you find any?

1-22 "DÉJÀ VU ALL OVER AGAIN"

More hair bloopers! Watch closely and you'll see Piper's hair go from a tidy up-do knot to a decidedly down-do with buckles—all with merely a turn of her head.

2-01 "WITCH TRIAL"

For your further consideration:

If the future is so witch-crazed, and Phoebe is a known witch, wouldn't *someone* notice when the windows suddenly blow out of Halliwell Manor one fine day?

2-02 "MORALITY BITES"

Did you catch the oogie-wires? The black cords are visible in the scene when Abraxas supposedly throws the sisters against the attic's far wall while stealing their *Book of Shadows*. The wires are used to drag the actors across the floor.

From time to time, the actors' tattoos, which are covered with makeup during filming, are inadvertently exposed; this time around, it's Holly Marie Combs's. Did you see it?

Wardrobe is caught out in a blooper this episode. A pink shirt in the final battle with Abraxas starts out whole but is soon sporting a significant tear—without reason!

For your further consideration:

Did they remodel the attic? The wall where Abraxas appeared *used* to have a small, round stained-glass window high in the peak that doesn't show up until the end of this episode. For that matter, when did the large windows opposite the doorway get flat across the top instead of rounded?

While Phoebe's motives are pure when she decides to allow herself to be burned, did she, or the other sisters, actually think that no one would notice two extra women in the execution chamber?

The *Book of Shadows* may open and close by itself (or with a little help from Grams), but the prop department let this blooper slip by. Despite making a point of there being no Return Spell in the future edition of the *Book of Shadows,* that page of the book is clearly visible, showing the exact images seen at the beginning of the episode, when the future Piper and Prue flip through it to remove the magical notes and components for their jail break.

Although Phoebe says, "We're back where we started" when the three sisters awaken in 1999, events don't repeat exactly. In the opening sequences, the instigating incident, the dog doing its business on the sidewalk, comes before the news report; in the closing sequences, the news report comes first and the doggie incident second.

2-03 "THE PAINTED WORLD"

The *Book of Shadows* is known to open to the relevant pages on occasion, but in this episode, it's *teleporting* other pieces of paper inside its cover. Watch where Phoebe puts the spell she's hiding—halfway through the book. When she goes to retrieve it, it's immediately inside the front cover! If you're even more observant, you'll also have noticed that the page marker ribbons, visible before the book is hidden, have mysteriously disappeared when Phoebe retrieves it from under the covers.

Fires are very localized in the *Charmed* world. Despite the fact that the painting was completely immolated, nothing except the painting is burned, not even the chair against which the painting was propped!

"Automatic door syndrome" is prevalent on *Charmed*, but this episode offers one of the better examples. Piper freezes Prue's assistant to retrieve the painting. When she enters the office, the door is open, but when she leaves with the painting, she has to open the door to escape.

2-04 "THE DEVIL'S MUSIC"

More inexplicable disappearances! Watch Piper's pearl necklace disappear from around her neck. Then observe the charm on Piper's necklace, which not only disappears but pops back in again—as does a *second* necklace she occasionally wears.

In the old days of film and television, boom microphones intruding on a scene were the bane of many a director. A scene in this episode illustrates a more modern version of the problem when the actress playing Piper leaves to answer an off-screen doorbell and reveals the black box of her portable microphone riding in the small of her back.

For your further consideration:

There's some sort of poetic justice working in that back room when the demon explodes. How else to explain that none of the witches closest to the demon, not even the women *inside* the demon, end up with as much demon slime on them as their hostile investor?

2-05 "SHE'S A MAN, BABY, A MAN!"
Phoebe evidently has a special power no one has noticed yet—the ability to sweat copiously without dampening any of her clothes!

For your further consideration:

If the succubus is supposed to be drawn to Prue (Mannie), how come she's already in the alley when Prue arrives? In Phoebe's vision, Darla watches Prue step outside—though Darla could have no way of knowing that's where Prue's sisters would direct her/him.

Any idea how the same blond woman manages to be standing directly behind all three sisters during the dance scene at the end of this program?

2-06 "THAT OLD BLACK MAGIC"
Why are the sisters so afraid of the snakes? *They* haven't been shrunk, and unless they had been, a constrictor (even a pair), wasn't going to do a full-grown woman any damage.

2-07 "THEY'RE EVERYWHERE"
For your further consideration:

When Piper is being held at knife point—with her hands completely free—why doesn't she freeze her attackers?

2-08 "P3 H2O"
There must be more stringent bus capacity rules at that camp than anywhere else. Although *three* buses arrive at the camp, Phoebe sprinkles powder on only a couple dozen kids. Who'd ever go Greyhound?

Necklaces and milk cartons aren't the only things disappearing around the sisters. In this episode, Piper runs toward the dock and yanks off her jacket, dropping it on the wharf. When she turns to run away, the jacket has gone missing.

2-09 "MS. HELLFIRE"
Did you spot any?

2-10 "HEARTBREAK CITY"
For your further consideration:

Why don't the sisters take the ring from Drazi while he's frozen the first time? Wouldn't it be so much tidier than trying to find it in the midst of all that demon sludge?

2-11 "RECKLESS ABANDON"
See anything interesting?

2-12 "AWAKENED"
For your further consideration:

Most fans couldn't help wondering just where the Halliwells find perfectly fitted size-two hospital gowns.

2-13 "ANIMAL PRAGMATISM"
For your further consideration:

How come the guys who are created from the rabbit and the pig don't choke on their collars when they become human? The collars are intended for much smaller necks.

2-14 "PARDON MY PAST"
Another disappearing-necklace scene! Watch Phoebe's purplish necklet during the action at the nursing home. See how it conveniently disappears before Anton hangs the antimagic amulet around her neck?

For your further consideration:

Anton merely drapes the necklace across Phoebe's neck as she lays on the bed; he doesn't lift her head to secure it. How is it latched when past-Phoebe sits up in the present?

2-15 "GIVE ME A SIGN"

Continuity errors aren't all that uncommon during filming, especially in scenes requiring special effects and multiple camera angles. In this episode's final confrontation, a number of torches are burning inside a crypt. Piper freezes the room. Torches from one angle are frozen; torches from the opposite viewpoint continue to dance.

For your further consideration:

Who replaces the camera lens cap between the time Prue snaps her self-portrait and Phoebe tries to nab some vibes from the dropped equipment?

Recalling how easily Prue magicked the ropes off Inspector Rodriguez in "Déjà Vu All Over Again," why doesn't she free herself when she bounces Bane Jessop into a wall?

2-16 "MURPHY'S LUCK"

Did you find anything?

2-17 "HOW TO MAKE A QUILT OUT OF AMERICANS"

For your further consideration:

It's a good thing Cryto doesn't actually manifest *inside* the circle when Aunt Gail and company summon him—there's no room, with all those candles.

Why does Prue say she "would" wear glasses if she needed them? She does wear glasses! Really cool cat glasses—the glasses she wore any number of times while examining artifacts at Bucklands.

2-18 "CHICK FLICK"

What was up with the red lighting in Prue's basement darkroom? Instead of bright room lighting, Finley was trying to assess Prue's prints in the dim red safe-lighting used to develop film and prints. When she was ready to attempt a second print of Finley, she turned *off* the dark room safe-lights and turned *on* the general room lights!

The clothes and prop blooper for "Chick Flick" occurs early in this episode. When Phoebe runs out of the house after the Demon of Illusion, she doesn't have a purse. Yet, when she gets to the theater, she's toting a bag big enough to be registered as a deadly weapon!

For a technical blooper, watch the final scenes in the theater. Although the film is projected onto the screen and Phoebe casts a shadow on the white wall, the film itself isn't projected onto Phoebe! That might work in a rear projection system, but not in the regular setup that allowed Prue to flick off the projector *behind the seats* and eliminate the bad guy.

For your further consideration:

Would Piper, a chef herself, really ask for the salt shaker *before* she'd even tasted the food?

What exactly was Prue doing with her negatives when she supposedly melted the image of her hero? The negative was in a tray that should be used in her enlarger. Instead, she has it under a magnifying light, a light normally used to view *prints*, and a light that would, in any case, use a bulb incapable of burning her film—probably a balanced white light, like a cool flourescent bulb.

2-19 "EX LIBRIS"

Did you spot any?

2-20 "ASTRAL MONKEY"

What do you think the chances are that all three sisters—as well as Dr. Williamson—were the same blood type? Unless due to some fantastic coincidence, there's no other explanation for the fact that Williamson and his monkeys didn't all die of blood mismatching!

Why did Prue spend so much time trying to convince her sisters that she saw a monkey? It's already been established that Prue works primarily in digital photography. The monkey was in the background of her photo of Evan Stone when she took his picture. Why didn't she just *show* instead of tell?

Incidental music, music added to the soundtrack of a television program, fades in and out throughout the show. But sounds on the set, like the blaring music in Benny Ritter's apartment, aren't supposed to do that unless someone turns them on or off. So, who turned off the music at Benny's while he and the doctor were rolling about on the floor?

For your further consideration:

Supposing that exposure to Halliwell blood is all it takes to pass along the powers, why didn't the girls gain one another's powers if, as Piper alludes when discussing her infected finger in "The Witch Is Back," they were all blood-brothers—or, rather, blood-sisters—at camp? (Will this plot device bring new meanings to "exchanges of bodily fluids" on *Charmed*? Do they now have to be careful who they bleed on? Did they actually all get to this age without ever donating blood? Does it mean they can never donate blood or be organ donors?) On a related note, did injection with Halliwell blood actually make the monkeys witches? Or was the fact that they didn't freeze when Williamson froze his boss, Jeffries, just another blooper?

2-21 "APOCALYPSE, NOT"

For your further consideration:

Okay, who, on being attacked by watermelon-tossing road-ragers, gets *out* of their car? Even if they can freeze time and orb out?

2-22 "BE CAREFUL WHAT YOU WITCH FOR"

Not really a blooper, but, did you notice all the wide wrist jewelry broken out for the last few episodes of the season? Must be easier on the skin, and quicker in wardrobe, than all the makeup that used to be used to hide the actresses' tattoos.

The

People
Who Charm

T. W. KING (Andy Trudeau), aka Theodore William King

Born: October 1, 1965, in Hollywood, California (raised in
Bethesda, Maryland)

Filmography:

Charmed Andy Trudeau (1998 – 99)

X-Files, FBI agent on roof (1998)

Timecop (TV series) Timecop Jack Logan (1997)

City, The (TV series) Danny Roberts (1995 – 97)

Loving (TV series) Danny Roberts (1995)

GREG VAUGHAN (Dan)

Born: June 15, 1975, in Dallas, Texas

Filmography:

Student Affairs (TV series) Jason (1999)

Charmed (TV series) Dan Gordon (1999 –)

Children of the Corn V: Fields of Terror Tyrus (1998)

No Small Ways (1997)

Poison Ivy: New Seduction Michael (1997)

Malibu Shores (TV series) Josh Walker (1996)

Beverly Hills, 90210 (TV series) Cliff Yeager (1996 – 97)

Casualty (1986) Jack Phillips; "Words and Deeds" 10/2/1999

Pacific Blue (1996) Trent Spence: "Broken Dreams" 12/6/1998

Mortal Kombat: Conquest (1998) Kebral; "Debt of the Dragon"
    11/13/1998

Love Boat (1998) Tom; "How Long Has This Been Going On?"
    5/4/1998

Legacy (1998)

Buffy the Vampire Slayer (1997) Richard Anderson: "Reptile Boy"
    10/13/1997

DORIAN GREGORY

Filmography:

Charmed (TV series) Darryl Morris (1998)

Just Write Valet at mansion party (1997)

Baywatch Nights (TV series) Tieg (1996 – 97)

Beverly Hills, 90210 Guard; "Home Is Where the Tart Is"
    9/13/1995

HOLLY MARIE COMBS

Born: December 3, 1973, in San Diego, California

Loves: Dogs! Cats! Horses! Pets!

Mom: Lauralei Combs

Sibs: None

Education: Professional Children's School, New York

Filmography:

Charmed (TV series) Piper Halliwell (1998)

Love's Deadly Triangle: The Texas Cadet Murder (TV movie) Diane Zamora (1997)

Daughters Alex Morrell (1997)

Sins of Silence (TV movie) Sophia DiMatteo (1996)

A Reason to Believe (TV movie) Sharon

Danielle Steel's "A Perfect Stranger" (TV movie) Amanda (1994)

Picket Fences (TV series) Kimberly Brock (1992)

Simple Men Kim (1992)

Chain of Desire Diana (1992)

Dr. Giggles Jennifer Campbell (1992)

Born on the Fourth of July Jenny (uncredited) (1989)

Sweet Hearts Dance Debs Boon (1988)

Relativity Anne Pryce (1997)

SHANNEN MARIA DOHERTY

Born: April 12, 1971, in Memphis, Tennessee

Mom: Rosa

Dad: Tom

Sibs: Older brother, Sean

Height: 5' 4"

Religious direction: Southern Baptist

Filmography:

Satan's School for Girls Beth/Karen Oxford (2000)

Striking Poses Gage Sullivan (1999)

Charmed Prue Halliwell (1998)

Shannen Doherty does have a few weaknesses besides horses; she confesses to owning more than two hundred and thirty pairs of shoes!

When looking for a model on which to build a male Prue
Halliwell in "She's a Man, Baby, a Man!," Shannen Doherty sup-
plied a picture of her current beau. Three hours, much makeup,
and a bodysuit later, she decided she wasn't nearly as good-
looking a man as a woman.

The Ticket (TV movie) CeeCee Reicker

Nowhere Val Chick 2 (1997)

Sleeping with the Devil Rebecca Dubrovich (1997)

Friend's 'Til the End Heather Romley (1997)

Gone in the Night Cindy Dowaliby (1996)

Mallrats Rene (1995)

A Burning Passion: The Margaret Mitchell Story Margaret Mitchell
(1994)

Jailbreakers (TV movie) Angel

Blindfold: Acts of Obsession Madeline Dalton (1994)

Almost Dead Katherine Roshak (1994)

Naked Gun 33 1/3: The Final Insult Herself
(uncredited) (1994)

Freeze Frame (TV movie) Lindsay Scott (1992)

Beverly Hills, 90210 Brenda Walsh (1990–94)

Heathers Heather Duke (1989)

Our House Kris Witherspoon (1986)

Outlaws (TV movie)

Girls Just Want to Have Fun Maggie Malene (1985)

Robert Kennedy and His Times (TV mini) Kathleen Kennedy (1985)

The Other Lover (TV movie) (1985)

Little House: The Last Farewell Jenny Wilder (1984)

Night Shift Bluebird (1982)

The Secret of NIMH (animated/voice) Teresa (1982)

Parker Lewis Can't Lose Herself; "Geek Tragedy" 4/12/1992

The Dennis Miller Show Herself (1992)

Life Goes On "Corky's Crush" 1/14/1990
21 Jump Street Janine; "Things We Said Today 12/18/1989
Highway to Heaven Shelley Fowler; "The Secret" 11/27/1985
Airwolf Phoebe Danner 9/8/1984
Magnum P.I. Ima Platt; "A Sense of Debt" 12/1/1983
Cagney and Lacey (1982)
Father Murphy Drusilla Shannon (1981)

ALYSSA JAYNE MILANO

Born: December 19, 1972, in Brooklyn, New York
Tattoos: 7. OM, the Hindu symbol for "peace" on her left wrist. One fairy on her hip. Rosary beads on her back. An angel on her left ankle, roses on the right. A sacred heart on her bottom. A cross on her back.
Loves: Horses! Hockey!
Mom: Lin
Dad: Tom
Sibs: Younger brother, Cory
Religious direction: Roman Catholic
Filmography:
  Buying the Cow (2000)
  Blink-182: The Urethra Chronicles Josie (1999)
  Jimmy Zip (1999)
  Charmed (TV series) Phoebe Halliwell
  Goldrush: A Real-life Alaskan Adventure (TV movie) Frances Ella
      Fitz (1998)
  Hugo Pool Hugo Dugay (1997)
  Body Count Susanne (1997) (Also producer)
  Melrose Place (TV series) Jennifer Mancini
      Campbell (1997 – 98)
  To Brave Alaska (TV movie) Denise Harris (1996)
  Glory Daze Chelsea (1996)
  No Fear Margo Masse (1996)
  Public Enemies Amaryllis (1996)

Though most fans can't imagine anyone else playing Phoebe Halliwell, Alyssa Milano *wasn't* the first choice for the role. The pilot was originally filmed with Lori Rom as the baby sister.

Deadly Sins Cristina (1995)

Poison Ivy II Lily (1995)

The Surrogate Amy Winslow (1995)

Embrace of the Vampire Charlotte (1994)

Candles in the Dark Sylvia Velliste (1993)

Casualties of Love: The Long Island Lolita Story (TV movie) Amy Fisher (1995)

Confessions of a Sorority Girl Rita (1993)

Conflict of Interest Eve (1993)

Double Dragon: The Movie Marian Delario (1993)

Webbers, The Fan (1993)

Little Sister Diana (1992)

Where the Day Takes You Kimmy (1992)

Cannonball Fever Truck driver (1989)

Dance 'Til Dawn Shelley Sheridan (1988)

Crash Course Vanessa Crawford (1988)

The Canterville Ghost (TV movie) Jennifer (1986)

Commando Jenny (1985)

Who's the Boss? (TV series) Samantha Micelli (1984)

Old Enough Diane (1984)

Fantasy Island Gina; "Superfriends" 10/3/1998

TRL Herself

Spin City Meg Watson; "They Shoot Horses, Don't They?" 12/10/1997

The Outer Limits Hannah Valesic; "Caught in the Act" 7/1/1995